People of the Dancing Sky

THE IROQUOIS WAY

PHOTOGRAPHS BY MYRON ZABOL

PROFILES BY LORRE JENSEN ~ FOREWORD BY TOM HILL

LYRICS PROVIDED BY ROBBIE ROBERTSON

Stoddart

Published in 2000 by Stoddart Publishing Co. Limited
34 Lesmill Road, Toronto, Canada M3B 2T6
180 Varick Street, 9th Floor, New York, New York 10014

Distributed by:
General Distribution Services Ltd.
325 Humber College Blvd., Toronto, Ontario M9W 7C3
Tel. (416) 213-1919   Fax (416) 213-1917
Email cservice@genpub.com

04 03 02 01 00   1 2 3 4 5

Canadian Cataloguing in Publication Data

Zabol, Myron
People of the dancing sky: the Iroquois way

Includes bibliographical references.

ISBN 0-7737-3247-0

1. Iroquois Indians — History. 2. Iroquois Indians — Biography. 3. Iroquois Indians — Portraits. I. Jensen, Lorre, 1941– . II. Title.

E99.I7Z32 2000   970'.0049755   C00-930724-9

Text and Jacket Design: Andrew Smith Graphics, Inc.
Color separation by Rainbow Digicolor Inc.,Toronto

All lyrics reprinted in this book were written by Robbie Robertson and used by permission of WB Music Corp. (ASCAP) & Medicine Hat Music (ASCAP). All rights administered by WB Music Corp. All rights reserved. WARNER BROS. PUBLICATIONS U.S. INC., Miami, FL 33014. Lyrics are drawn from the following songs: "The Code of Handsome Lake" © 1998; "Ghost Dance" © 1995; "Golden Feather" © 1995; "Holy Hell" © 1998; "In the Blood" © 1998; "It Is a Good Day to Die" © 1995; "The Lights" © 1998; "Making a Noise" © 1998; "Pray" © 1998; "Rattlebone" © 1998; "Skinwalker" © 1995; "Stomp Dance (Unity)" © 1998; "Unbound" © 1998.

The people and artwork pictured on pages iv–26 and 108 are identified as follows. All photographs by Myron Zabol: page iv, Jim Sky; page vi, Cody, Jack, and Delsun Moore; page xi, Tia Smith; page xii, False Face mask by Craig Longboat; page 3, carving by David Maracle; page 4, carving of The Great Peace Tree by Leroy Hill; page 5, pottery by Steven Smith; page 8, Hadui carving by Craig Longboat; page 9, rattles carved by Fred Williams; page 10, Stan Hill with his moose antler carving, "The Great Peace Tree"; page 14, corn husk mask, artist unknown; page 21, Steven Raymond Johnson, a Tuscarora of the Turtle Clan; page 23, Jim Sky demonstrating use of a Snow Snake; page 25, Cody Moore; page 26, Margaret Bomberry Key, a Mohawk of the Turtle Clan; page 108, Quentin Pipestem. Pages 2, 6, 7, 11–13, and 15–20 feature scenes at Crawford Lake Indian Village in Ontario.

We acknowledge for their financial support of our publishing program the Canada Council for the Arts, the Ontario Arts Council, and the Government of Canada through the Book Publishing Industry Development Program (BPIDP).

Printed and bound in Canada

To Jim Sky
TEACHER
Whose words embrace the spirit of his people

CONTENTS

FOREWORD

The people in these resplendent photographs by Myron Zabol remind us all that the culture and traditions of North America's Native peoples are alive and well and adapting wholeheartedly to changing times, without losing their distinctiveness. Dressed in their "Indian" clothes, these people are a living legacy, demonstrating that conformity to the whiteman's world is far removed from their trains of thought. Poised and confident, the stature of these Iroquoian dancers, performers, and community leaders and members is eternal and unwavering.

At the beginning of the twentieth century, many Iroquoians were bound to rigid community standards that determined their dress. Followers of the traditional Longhouse subscribed to a code of behavior that did not encourage individuality. But with the advent of the pow-wow in Iroquoia, community standards changed and, like culture, dress has undergone enormous modifications in the past twenty years.

Many contemporary Iroquoians have a pow-wow outfit and not a *Gus-to-wa* (headdress), *Ga-Ka'-ah* (kilt), *Gise-ha* (leggings), *Ah-ta-qua-oh-weh* (moccasins), and *Ga-geh-ta* (belt). Look at Amos Key's portrait, for instance. Amos Key is a faithkeeper in the Seneca Longhouse and lead singer of the Old Mush Singers singing society, but he is also a champion traditional pow-wow dancer. A bustle of eagle feathers, an eagle sun visor, a satin shirt, an eagle-head dance staff, and elaborate beaded leggings, kilt, and vest make up his pow-wow kit. He is no less a Haudenosaunee for all this. Much ingenuity and many tastes are displayed in the execution of the pow-wow outfit, which makes Amos Key the proud dancer, with his emphasis on proving his worth and showing how intricately he is dressed. In fact, opulence and ornamentation are the norm — even excess is considered good.

The pow-wow is not the only influence on contemporary Iroquoian ceremonial dress. Ironically, but to great creative benefit, some outfits have roots in turn-of-the-century Wild West shows like *101 Ranch* and *Buffalo Bill's Wild West Show*. Many Iroquoian and other Native families joined these traveling shows as a way of earning a living — and they adopted a style of dress more dependent on what they did in the show than on their own traditions. The Sioux war bonnet and the ribbon shirt grew out of this history. Jimmy Sky, an Onondaga faithkeeper, stands erect, drumming a western-style drum and staring out beyond the frame of the photo. He is dressed in a ribbon shirt, but it is clear that he also wants to be identified as Iroquoian — through his headdress, his intricately beaded moccasins, his deer-toe armbands, and his leggings. Fred Williams also poses in western-influenced regalia —

complete with bull whip — for an act he performed in Wild West shows. He learned from his father, Fred Williams, Sr., who rode in the original Buffalo Bill production.

Women's outfits have also evolved and borrowed from other Native groups. The traditional outfit is a cloth dress, an underskirt, and leggings made from British stroud, embellished with lace, beadwork, and ribbon. Although the pow-wow has had a profound and lasting influence, it is fashion designers who have revamped and integrated new elements into the women's dress. In the exquisite portrait of Christina Bomberry, this young woman looks directly into the camera lens, with her hands on her hips and an infectious smile. Her provocative look is more reflective of fashion photography than portraiture. And her longer fringe and contemporary beadwork, combined with a headpiece reminiscent of a fifteenth-century Iroquoian crown — with a fashionable flow of feathers — present viewers with a challenge: She is Haudenosaunee but she can still use other traditions to create elegance and grace.

The images in this book seem to be more than photographs. Myron Zabol's black and white photos interweave themselves into our thoughts and imaginations. From the beginning of the project, Zabol's goal was to establish a body of work illustrating the traditional Longhouse people as they were in the 1990s.

The Haudenosaunee carry many beliefs and traditions, but none is more appropriate to this book than the doctrine of *Gas-gon-yonh*. It is a speech of encouragement, which states that you must have your traditional clothes ready, in order to make your journey to the Spirit World. Look at the photo of Chief Peter Sky sitting in the rocking chair — he is ready.

Tom Hill
Six Nations Territory
February 2000

ACKNOWLEDGMENTS

My deepest appreciation goes to the Haudenosaunee People of the Six Nations Confederacy for allowing me to embrace their society. I began this project in 1995 with the intention of recording the lives and traditions of the Haudenosaunee (Iroquois) People of Canada and the United States at the end of the twentieth century. Over time, however, as the work progressed, it became more than a photographic enterprise. With great interest I watched the story of the Native Way, with the Iroquois beliefs in Nature and things ancient, unfold before me. The journey was spiritual, magical, and most profound. The Haudenosaunee People, simply put, are quite special.

The body of work in this book reflects the way these people are today. Their traditional Longhouse society and beliefs are intact, and they have more than retained their spirituality and individuality in modern times. The title *People of the Dancing Sky* is my allusive interpretation of what they meant to me. Although the Haudenosaunee do not refer to themselves in this way, their spirit and their love of life brought this name to mind.

My deepest gratitude goes to Jim Sky, his wife Deanna, and their family. Jim Sky, an Onondaga faithkeeper, was not only my spiritual guide but also a companion to me as I carried out my work. His vision and deep-rooted wisdom kept me on a defined journey for years while photographing the Iroquois Way of Life.

A special word of thanks to Amos Key, who provided valuable information about Longhouse beliefs and ceremonies and reviewed the introduction in great detail. Amos is a faithkeeper at Six Nations and is employed as Language Program Director at the Woodlands Cultural Centre in Brantford. Thanks also go to George Beaver, who provided the initial research and writing for the introduction.

I would also like to thank Tom Hill, the Mohawk Curator of the Woodlands Cultural Centre, for his insightful foreword and for his assistance with the project.

Deepest appreciation goes to Lorre Jensen, Director of Education at the National Aboriginal Achievement Foundation, and a Mohawk, for providing sensitive and intriguing written profiles for the people photographed. As she prepared the profiles, she embarked on a profound journey back to her own Native Way.

I would also like to acknowledge Bruce Chalmers and Peter Kruka of Agfa Canada and Agfa Germany for their ongoing support and never-failing belief in my photographic work.

To Robbie Robertson, whom I met very briefly at his "Honoring Dance" at the Six Nations Pow-Wow in 1997, my deepest gratitude for his support, as well as for the lyrics from *Music for the Native Americans* and *Contact from the Underworld of Red Boy*, which give the pages additional character.

To my daughter, Nevada, and my wife, Shirley, I owe a great deal of gratitude for your understanding and for your belief, in allowing me to develop this project.

To Andrew Smith, thank you for your wonderful book design, which displays the photographs to great advantage, and to Kathryn Dean at Wordscapes Associates, for your editing, research, and polishing of the profiles and the introduction. Finally, I express my great appreciation to Nelson Doucet and his team at Stoddart Publishing for their belief in, and professional handling of, the manuscript that became *People of the Dancing Sky*.

MYRON ZABOL
TORONTO, CANADA
FEBRUARY 2000

THE HAUDENOSAUNEE ~ THE IROQUOIS
"PEOPLE OF THE LONGHOUSE"

MOHAWK
Kanyekehala "People of the Flint"

CAYUGA
Kayahkhana "People of the Portage"

ONEIDA
Oneyoteka "People of the Standing Stone"

SENECA
Onotowaka "People of the Big Hill"

ONONDAGA
Onotakeka "People of the Village on the Hill"

TUSCARORA
Dahsgao:we "People of the Long Shirts"

IN THE
BEGINNING

THIS BOOK of photographs celebrates the culture and accomplishments of the Iroquois, or Haudenosaunee, people. The portraits fix in time moments of late-twentieth-century life among the Iroquois of southern Ontario, Quebec, and upstate New York — but they also reflect traditions that have their roots in earlier eras. Their domains once stretched across the northern part of present-day New York State — from the Genesee River on the west, through the Finger Lakes, and to the Hudson River on the east. Linguistically related to the neighboring

Huron, Petun, and Attiwandaron, the Iroquois were nevertheless distinct, and by the fifteenth or sixteenth century, they had formed the Five Nations Confederacy — an alliance of the Seneca, Cayuga, Onondaga, Oneida, and Mohawk nations — in order to defend the peace in Iroquois territory. In 1724, the Tuscarora joined, creating the Six Nations.[*] Known as the Haudenosaunee, the Six Nations people were called the Iroquois by the French — and that name has passed into common usage.

The stability of the Iroquois Confederacy derived from a strong farming economy controlled by the women and from their federal constitution, known as the Great Law of Peace, which governed the affairs of all five nations.[**] Central to the Confederacy's workings was the idea and reality of the Longhouse, which had (and still has today) ceremonial, social, and political purposes. The long-house was, literally, a dwelling which housed an extended family, headed by a clan mother. But over time the longhouse as a structure became a symbol taking on political and spiritual significance: Each Iroquoian nation had its own central Longhouse, where their council met to make political decisions and where religious ceremonies were held to give thanks to the Creator and to appoint the community's spiritual and political leaders.

The business of each community is carried out in the Longhouse by *raianer* (Mohawk Confederacy statesmen, or hereditary chiefs), who have been nominated and appointed by a matriarch (or clan mother), who represents the clan in the appointing process. Then they are ratified by the chiefs through an elaborate ceremony of condolence. In the pages that follow, you will see the terms *chief, sachem, peace chief, hereditary chief,* and *raianer* — all of which are used in English to refer to these political legislators/leaders of the Confederacy Council. *Raianer* is the original Mohawk term, and the other five nations use similar terms.

* Geoffrey York and Loreen Pindera, *People of the Pines: The Warriors and the Legacy of Oka* (Toronto: Little, Brown, 1991), p. 147.   **Ibid., p. 145.

Although the spiritual and political aspects of life are often not separated in Iroquoian culture, the *faithkeepers* of the Longhouse have the greatest responsibility in preserving and passing on the spiritual belief systems. These men and women conduct and organize the ceremonies in the Longhouse, teaching the beliefs through the ceremonies — having been chosen by the various clans and presented in a Longhouse meeting, where they are charged with their serious task by a group of clans called a *moiety*. "The Creator is watching and listening," a *moiety* representative might say on the momentous day when a faithkeeper is appointed. "And the people are looking to you for help and guidance." No one may ask to be a faithkeeper, and no one chosen by the *moiety* may decline to be a faithkeeper, as their role has been preordained by the Creator.

Each spiritual Longhouse has two *moieties*, and each *moiety* has two leaders, one male and one female faithkeeper. These leaders must have an intricate understanding of how the ceremonies are to be carried out, and they are usually the speakers, as well — but not always. Anyone with a gift of leadership and ability in public speaking could be appointed to the role of speaker on any given occasion.

Longhouse ceremonies are held for people to give thanks to the Creator or to mark the changing seasons and critical events in their lives: marriage, birth, death. The ceremonies include a wide array of dancing, music, song, and orations. The orations — speeches about Iroquoian history and social and political laws — are carried out by the Longhouse speaker and may last for days. The tenets of the oration must be memorized, an almost impossible feat, but one that is mastered by many, sometimes with the help of a mnemonic device. The most common memory aid is a belt or string made with great care from shell beads, or wampum, of natural colors. They include designs that represent important occasions, agreements, and covenants. One of the best-known of the wampum is the Two-Row Wampum Treaty belt, which represents the agreement made between the Europeans and the Iroquoian Confederacy. Its white background represents the social context, the land, and the resources shared by both societies. The dark purple beads represent two rows of canoes, indicating that the two societies are to live together in harmony, without interfering with each other by enacting and imposing laws on each other.

Many ceremonies are mentioned in the pages to come, but those most frequently described include the Midwinter Ceremonies, the Naming Ceremony, and the Condolence Ceremony. The Midwinter Ceremonies are most often held beginning on the fifth night after the New Moon in January. They last for no fewer than eight days and consist of many different renewal ceremonies — all related to the ending of one ceremonial year and the beginning of a new one: the Stirring

Ashes Ceremony (of thanksgiving and symbolic cleansing), the Renewal of Ceremonial Medicines, and the Four Great Thanksgiving Ceremonies. The Four Great Thanksgiving Ceremonies (*Gei Niyoihawage*) include dance, music, tobacco invocations, and a clan game: the Great Feather Dance (*Ostowahgo:wa*), the Drum Dance (*Ganèho:*), the Personal Male Songs (*Adó:wa*), and the Great Dish Game (*Gayedowá:neh*). During this time the Naming Ceremony is also celebrated. In this ceremony, babies born since the fall receive the name of an ancestor — one chosen by a clan mother or the maternal grandmother, from names belonging to the clan.

On other occasions, the longhouse is the scene of social gatherings where people participate in social music and dances. The social dance repertoire can include as many as twenty social dances. These do not have the spiritual significance of the ceremonial dances, but they are unique to the Iroquoian community and a source of great entertainment, though they are not easily mastered. Unlike the ceremonial dances, which cannot be rendered in front of the general public, the social dances are open for all to see — and they are performed by dance groups and companies at exhibitions, public performances, and dance festivals.

In the seventies and eighties, as travel between communities became easier for the First Nations, some Iroquoian people began adopting the dances that had traditionally been practiced only by the First nations of the Prairies, at pow-wows. Since the pow-wows evolved to include dancing competitions, some Longhouse people felt that the Longhouse people who adopted the pow-wow-style dances distorted and diluted an important tenet — the Iroquoian view that a person's dancing ability is a gift from the Creator to be exercised with a great deal of humility. Still, many Longhouse people who embraced the western pow-wow dances and incorporated them into their own traditional repertoire were always mindful of the fact that the pow-wow dances they adopted could still be executed with the same mastery, integrity, and humility as the Longhouse social and ceremonial dances.

Some of the people featured in these photos are known as condoled chiefs. They are hereditary chiefs, or *raianer*, and like their ancestors, they have been appointed by the clan mothers specifically to replace a chief who has passed on or has become incapacitated and so unable to fulfill the duties required in representing the clan. When a chief dies, the state enters a ten-day mourning period and the remaining chiefs conduct a small, private condolence ceremony for the family and relatives of the bereaved. The clan mother, her family, and her clan will then appoint a new chief to carry out the necessary duties until such time as the new chief can be ratified by a Grand Council. This ratification is popularly known as the Condolence Ceremony and will be held at a Grand Council meeting, where several new chiefs and clan mothers may be condoled, or appointed, to replace *raianer* and clan mothers who have passed away.

The Longhouse as a religion was intricate and highly organized when the Europeans first arrived in North America, and despite the social upheaval and the religious and political persecution of its adherents, it remains strong today. As a result of being pushed to the margins of society, there was a time when the Longhouse religious practices were not carried out as openly. Today, however, the ceremonies are enjoying a renaissance, and the people of the community are participating in and enjoying the religious practices with renewed vigor.

The historic geographical base of the Iroquois in upstate New York has also shifted and expanded. After the American Revolution, many of the Six Nations formally adopted a tract of land in southern Ontario in a deal made with Sir Frederick Haldimand, governor of Quebec, and brokered by Joseph Brant, a Mohawk. The tract extended six miles on either side of the Grand River, from its mouth to its source. The area was reduced over the years to mere acres, and much of it remains under land claims. The remaining portion still exists as the Six Nations Territory near Brantford, Ontario. Many of those whose photos appear in this book live at Six Nations, but communities elsewhere in Ontario, Canada, and in New York State are also featured here. In Canada, there are several major Iroquois communities apart from Six Nations: the Oneida settlement near London, Ontario; Akwesasne south of Cornwall, Ontario, which straddles the borders of Ontario, Quebec, and New York State; Kahnawake, southwest of Montreal; Kanesatake, near the town of Oka, west of Montreal; Wahta near Bala, Ontario; and Tyendinaga on the Bay of Quinte, near Belleville, Ontario.

In New York State, the Tuscarora live on a reservation between Lewiston and Sanborn, northeast of Niagara Falls. The Seneca have three communities: Cattaraugus, near Irving, New York, along the shore of Lake Erie, Allegheny at Salamanca (south of Cattaraugus), and the Tonawanda reservation near Akron, New York. The Oneida are centered around Verona, east of Albany; the Onondaga are just outside of Syracuse; and the Mohawk are at Akwesasne, which includes the island of St. Regis in the St. Lawrence River. The Cayuga reservation was expropriated in past years, so this nation is now housed with the Seneca. There is also an Oneida reservation near Green Bay, Wisconsin, and Seneca and Cayuga communities in the State of Oklahoma.

Throughout the Iroquoian communities in Canada and the United States, there are two systems of government: the traditional Confederacy councils and the elected councils, established and sometimes imposed by the federal Canadian and American governments. In Canada, elected councils are known as band councils; in the United States they are known as tribal councils.

Generally, in Canada, each community has both systems of government, whereas in the United States the Iroquoian communities are usually governed by either the Longhouse or an elected council, but not both.

Iroquois society and the Confederacy have faced great challenges over the past three centuries, but they have never extinguished their rights, and they have remained strong by passing on their languages, institutions, customs, traits, and histories. The following brief historical overview will give you a sense of Iroquois life, past and present, through the Iroquois Creation Story, the Great Law of Peace, the vision of the Iroquois prophet Handsome Lake, and the lives of present-day artists and performers. First, here is one version of the Creation Story — the account of how it all began.

THE IROQUOIS CREATION STORY:
THE WOMAN WHO FELL FROM THE SKY WORLD

In the beginning there was a Sky World. In the middle of that Sky World grew a Great Tree of Light, which everyone was supposed to take care of. But one day a woman who was expecting a baby asked her husband to dig around the Tree to see if there were any tasty roots to eat because she had a craving for different food.

After he had dug a deep hole, the woman thought she saw something at the bottom. So she leaned far down into the hole, and to her surprise, she saw not roots but a whole other world,

completely covered with water. Her husband scrambled out of the way, and she leaned far down, to get a better look. Then she slipped and fell through the hole, clutching at the plants growing around the Tree as she went.

The birds flying above the water noticed her first. The wild geese flew up to catch her in their strong wings, while other birds flew off to ask a huge turtle swimming nearby if the Sky Woman could be placed on its back. The turtle gave permission, and the woman, still holding plants from the Sky World between her fingers, was placed on the turtle's back.

The birds and water animals then began to take turns diving, in an attempt to bring up some soil for the plants the woman had brought with her. One after the other, they all failed to reach the bottom. At last, only the humble muskrat was left, and some of the other creatures laughed when he said he wanted to try, but he dived down anyway. After a long time, he floated to the surface unconscious, but in his paws he was clutching some mud.

This tiny bit of soil was placed on the turtle's back, and as the Sky Woman walked around it, the bit of soil grew and grew. In due time, the Sky Woman gave birth to a daughter, and the two females went on making Turtle Island grow bigger and bigger by walking around it.

THE GOOD TWIN AND THE EVIL-MINDED TWIN

The Sky Woman's daughter grew up to be a beautiful young woman. One day as she lay sleeping among the trees and plants which her mother had brought from the Sky World, she was seen by the Spirit of the West Wind. This powerful spirit, who just happened to be passing by, was arrested by the sight of the gorgeous maiden and deeply stirred. He determined that she would bear him twin sons. As a sign of this, he placed two arrows on her stomach. One arrow was sharp and one was blunt.

Even before they were born, the twins struggled with each other in their mother's womb. When it was time for their delivery, the right-handed twin was born normally, but the left-handed twin insisted on coming out under his mother's arm, which eventually killed her. This evil little fellow even convinced his grandmother that it was his good and upright brother, the right-handed twin, who had caused their mother's death. For this reason, he became his grandmother's favorite, in spite of the fact that he always got into mischief and caused trouble.

The twins' grandmother tenderly buried their mother, and from the grave grew corn, beans, and squash — which gave birth to the phrase "the Three Sisters." These later became three of the main foods grown by the Five Nations Iroquois. The Woman Who Fell from the Sky then named the left-handed twin Sawiskera (Mischievous One) and the right-handed twin Teharonhiawakon (Holder of the Heavens).

After their grandmother died, the good twin wanted to give her a proper burial, but the bad twin wanted to just kick her body off the edge of the world. These two powerful beings then fought over her body. The evil-minded twin succeeded in snatching off her head, and he hurled it far into space. Most people now call it the moon, but in Ceremonies, it is still referred to as "our Grandmother" by the Haudenosaunee.

The good twin finally succeeded in burying his grandmother properly. Then he set about to create all sorts of beautiful things, such as flowers, birds, and butterflies. However, the evil twin tried to spoil his brother's beautiful creations as much as possible. When the good twin made roses, Sawiskera put thorns on them. When he created beautiful deer, his evil brother made fierce mountain lions to prey upon them.

At last the day came when they decided to have a contest to see who would be the ruler of the world. They played lacrosse, but after six days, the game ended in a draw. So they finally agreed to a fight to the finish, using only one weapon each. Sawiskera chose a spear as his weapon and his brother picked deer antlers. The evil-minded twin used every dirty trick he could think of, but his brother always fought fair. For several days they fought evenly. At last the right-handed twin realized that he, too, would have to resort to trickery. He began to pretend to be tiring. Sawiskera thought he was winning and grew careless. Suddenly the right-handed twin caught him and threw him down on the sharp deer antlers. Sawiskera was unable to continue. He had lost the contest.

The good twin did not kill his brother. Instead, he let him become the ruler of the night, while he became the ruler of the day.

TEHARONHIAWAKON (HOLDER OF THE HEAVENS) MEETS HADUI (HA-DOO-EE)

With the evil-minded twin banished to the night, the good twin went about unhindered, finishing his beautiful work of Creation. One day as he traveled about, he was surprised to see another man-

like being sitting on a rock, looking around. The good-minded twin knew about his father, the Spirit of the West Wind, and he had suspected that other spirits might also dwell on the earth. Now, here was one powerful enough to assume an almost-human form. He went forward to ask what manner of being this stranger was.

"I am the creator of all that you see around you," he told Teharonhiawakon, "and who are you?"

The good-minded twin told him who he was and added that it was actually he who had created all the beautiful things on earth. When this spirit being expressed doubt, the good twin realized that they must settle this with a test. He proposed that they turn their backs to a distant mountain. Each one would try to move the mountain closer. The one who moved the mountain closest would be declared the real Creator.

The stranger went first. He shook his great turtle rattle and summoned the mountain. With a loud roar of crashing rocks, the mountain moved forward a bit. Then Teharonhiawakon commanded the mountain to come forward, and the stranger thought he felt something at his back. He quickly whirled around and smashed his face against the mountain, which was now right behind him. There was no doubt about who the real Creator was and who was most powerful.

"I am beaten," said the man-like being, "but I still have great power. I do not want to be banished from this earth. If you let me stay, I promise to help the people who are still to come. Your people will carve masks in my likeness to remind them of this occasion and of my promise to cure the sick and drive out evil spirits."

This was the beginning of the Medicine Mask Society. In later years, the Iroquois called this spirit being Hadui (Ha-doo-ee), and when they carved his likeness, they usually added a large, crooked nose on his face, to remind people of his contest with the Creator.

THE CREATION OF PEOPLE

When he had made enough plants, animals, birds, and fish, the Creator decided it was time to make some creatures in his own likeness. He formed the first group from the bark of a tree, the second group from the white foam of the sea, the third group from black soil, and the fourth from red earth. They each turned out to have a different color of skin.

After a while, the four groups of human beings began to fight with each other. The Creator thought they might not survive if they kept this up, so he separated them. He took the yellow, white, and black-skinned humans across the salt water and placed them far away from each other. He left the red-skinned humans at their place of origin, which was Turtle Island (North America).

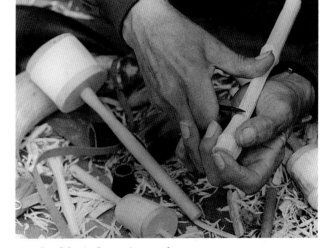

THE GREAT MIGRATIONS OF THE PRE-IROQUOIS PEOPLE

The Creation Story stops here. We pick up the thread again through linguistic studies, which indicate that in ancient times, the Haudenosaunee, or Iroquois, as they were called by the French, may have been one people with a single language. However, they eventually split into many different groups before the Mohawk, the Oneida, the Onondaga, the Cayuga, and the Seneca formed a Confederacy in the fifteenth or sixteenth century.

The group who became the Tuscarora traveled west to Lake Erie, then southeast to the Allegheny River. Here one group stopped, while the others crossed to the other side of the river. Those who remained became known by various names, including the Andaste and the Conestoga. Those who left continued south to the Roanoke and Neuse rivers, in what today is North Carolina, and became the Tuscarora. According to Tuscarora historian David Cusick, the Eries after whom Lake Erie is named were thought to be a branch of the Seneca Nation. They lived west of the Seneca along the southern shores of Lake Erie.

THE *GAYAN̲EHSRAGOWAH* (THE GREAT LAW OF PEACE):
THE FEDERAL CONSTITUTION OF THE LONGHOUSE PEOPLE

Perhaps as long as a thousand years ago, the Five Nations were at war with each other and with other, nearby nations. Blood feuds between families were rife, and war chiefs had great power and prestige. One of the most feared of the war chiefs was Tadodaho of the Onondaga nation. A rival leader, Hai:watha — a man of peace — was persecuted so much by Tadodaho that he left the Onondagas and went east to live among the Mohawk.

There he met a man who came to be called Deganawida, the Peacemaker. He had spent many years traveling among the Five Nations, carrying a message of peace and unity. He recruited Hai:watha and a woman named Jigonsaseh to help him. Jigonsaseh's house was located on the Warriors' Path, and she fed and housed travelers, mainly men on their way to war. This gave her

a unique opportunity to tell them of the Peacemaker's vision of a just and peaceful society. Giving up her profitable profession, she even traveled to the land of the Onondaga to help the Peacemaker and Hia:watha at the first Grand Council — the founding council of the Five Nations Confederacy.

Hai:watha was a powerful and persuasive speaker, who helped the less fluent Peacemaker immensely. Most people believe the Peacemaker was a Huron, born north of Lake Ontario near the Bay of Quinte — which would account for his lack of fluency in the Five Nations' languages. The Peacemaker thought out the complex concepts of the Great Law of Peace, and Hai:watha acted as his voice. (He is called the Peacemaker because to use his real name, Deganawida, in casual conversation is considered too disrespectful.) He believed he was sent by the Creator, and his deeds indicated that he had great spiritual power.

The Peacemaker and Hai:watha labored for years, gradually building support as they traveled back and forth among the Five Nations. With the help of Jigonsaseh, they created a Confederacy based on peace and unity of mind.

The Great Law of Peace is the constitution of a stable, democratic government. It contains a complex system of checks and balances between the rights and powers of men and women, of young and old, of clans and nations. It made the Five Nations one family, living in a symbolic Longhouse. This ensured peace, since one did not wage war with family members.

SYMBOLS OF THE GREAT LAW OF PEACE

The Peacemaker used several symbols to help people remember the concepts of the Great Law: the Tree of Peace, the bundle of arrows, and the bowl and the beaver's tail. According to oral tradition, the *Tree of Peace* was tipped over and weapons were thrown into the hole. The tree was then set back upright, burying weapons forever. It had four great white roots, which reached out to the four directions. Any individual or nation who wished to seek shelter could follow one of the roots to peace and security under the Tree of Peace.

The *bundle of arrows* symbolized strength in unity. Each nation gave the Peacemaker one arrow. He then tied them together into a strong bundle and warned that if any of the Five Nations removed their arrow, they would weaken the power of the Confederacy. The bundle signified that all the people of the Confederacy had become united as one person. The *bowl and the beaver's tail* made reference to the hunting grounds of the Five Nations. The Peacemaker took one large bowl and placed a cooked beaver's tail in it. The bowl represented the hunting grounds, which would be held in common. No knife was placed in it, so no one would be cut when they reached in. This signified that all danger of shedding blood was removed. There was now an international council (the Grand Council) to settle any disputes over the hunting ground. Chiefs from all of the Five Nations participated in this council to discuss matters affecting the entire Confederacy.

CLANS AND LONGHOUSES

The Grand Council was based on a matrilineal system of order, which gave rise to the Iroquoian clan system. All Iroquois belonged not only to their nation but also to a clan. The clans were not subcategories of the Longhouse but, rather, family ties that cut across all long-houses and all nations. Membership in a clan depended on the mother's lineage, and any clan member among the Mohawks, for example, was regarded as a relative of every member of the same clan within any of the other Five Nations. People of the same clan could not marry each other. Three of the clans had members in all five of the nations: the Bear Clan, the Turtle Clan, and the Deer Clan. Other clans existed in some of the nations, but not all five (usually, they extended across three or four). These clans were the Wolf, the Hawk, the Heron, the Snipe, the Beaver, and the Eel. The clan system helped maintain peace, since members of a clan were like brothers and sisters, and family members were not allowed to fight each other.

THE CLAN MOTHERS

Each clan mother lived in a longhouse with her extended family. As her daughters married, the longhouse was extended and new apartments were added at either end. Old-time longhouses were comparable in size to a barn, only longer. People slept with their feet toward the centre, on low

platforms, covered with furs and blankets. The space below the high ceiling was filled with strings of drying corn — and tobacco, since it was believed that the Creator loved the smell of tobacco. Medicinal plants, beans, dried bark, venison, and other provisions also hung below the rafters. The longhouse was the domain of the mothers, while the forest was the domain of the men.

The longhouse set-up meant that aunts and uncles, grandmothers and grandfathers, and older cousins were always nearby and could take care of the children if their parents were too busy or if one or both had died. Each family in the longhouse had a firepit, where a large pot of soup simmered all day, ready for hungry children or adults.

The longhouse was also a place of shelter for "the coming faces" — the unborn generations of Iroquois. These "faces coming from the ground" needed a safe and healthy environment in which to grow during their tender years.

THE COUNCILS AND THE IMPORTANCE OF WOMEN IN IROQUOIS SOCIETY

The clan mothers did much more than act as heads of their own longhouses, however. They also nominated members of their extended family to sit on the governing councils. The clan mother would nominate the most suitable candidate in her family — and that nomination would be confirmed by all the clan mothers. These candidates, called the *raianer* (sachems, or peace chiefs), formed a council that dealt with their nation's issues. (There were also subchiefs who sat on local village councils.) If a clan mother felt that any *raianer* had lost the confidence and respect of the clan, she could depose him and select a replacement. Whenever a *raianer* was deposed or had died, a new one was appointed, or "condoled," to the Longhouse Council through a ceremony that included a rite of condolence for the dead.[*]

Some believe that the Longhouse of each nation was led by a war chief as well as a council of peace chiefs. Whether any war chiefs had clout in the Longhouse is not certain, but there were definitely war chiefs who made military decisions.[**]

[*] York and Pindera, pp. 147–48. [**]Ibid.

THE *RAIANER*

The English word "chief" is not a good translation for the Mohawk word *raianer*, for the idea of the *raianer* embodied not only nobility but also holiness. "No matter what nature of question or business may come before you, no matter how sharp and aggravating," the Peacemaker said to the first *raianer*, "it will not penetrate your skin. You will . . . never disgrace yourself by becoming angry. You . . . shall always be guided in all your councils by the good tidings of Peace and Power." His charge to the *raianer* showed that they would be carrying on the Creator's work.

THE GRAND COUNCIL, OR CONFEDERACY COUNCIL

The *raianer* dealt not just with village or national issues. Some also sat on the Grand Council, or Confederacy Council, that dealt with matters affecting the entire Confederacy. The eight clans

of the Seneca presented eight candidates for *raianer* to the Confederacy Council; the eight clans of the Cayuga presented ten; the eight clans of the Onondaga presented fourteen; the three clans of the Oneida presented nine; and the three clans of the Mohawk presented nine. This made a total of fifty candidates for the fifty positions of *raianer* on the council.

The Five Nations Confederacy was like the United Nations. No nation lost any freedom but kept running its own affairs, speaking its own language and following its own customs and the religions of its people's choice. When questions of national interest arose, a clan brought it before its own nation's fire (or council) for discussion. If it was an internal matter, a decision was made at that level. A question that involved other nations was then presented to the international body — the Confederacy Council of all the Five Nations. The Elder Brothers (the Seneca and the Mohawk) would discuss the issue and come to a consensus. The Younger Brothers (the Cayuga and the Oneida) would then see if they could come to a similar consensus. If they did, the matter was ratified by the Keepers of the Central Fire, the Onondaga. If the Onondaga did not agree, the matter was sent back until a better solution was worked out.

THE FIRST CONFEDERACY COUNCIL

One of the Mohawk candidates to the first Confederacy Council was none other than Hai:watha himself, who had long since been adopted by the Mohawk people. Tadodaho, a famous Onondaga, whose tale will be told below, was a candidate as well. The Peacemaker refused to allow his own name to be put forward by any nation for the position of *raianer*. "There shall be no successor to my title," he said, "and no man shall be called by my name." That is why there is never a "Deganawida" listed among the fifty names of the *raianer*.

A LONGHOUSE OF ONE MIND

The Five Nations regarded their vast territory as a huge longhouse, which stretched across the five Finger Lakes (the Creator was said to have scratched them out with his fingers). The Seneca nation were the Keepers of the Western Door, and the Mohawk were the Keepers of the Eastern Door. Like each family in a physical longhouse, each nation had a fire, or council. In the middle of this idealized longhouse were the Onondaga, who were the Keepers of the Central Fire ("the Fire That Never Dies.")

TADODAHO: WARLORD AND SORCERER

The story of the formation of the Confederacy of the Five Nations (also known as the League of Five Nations) would not be complete without telling about the fearsome Onondaga war chief Tadodaho (Ta-doh-da-ho). Tadodaho was not only a great war leader in the never-ending conflicts

among the Five Nations before the time of the Great Law of Peace; he was also said to have been a sorcerer, who could do away with his enemies using witchcraft. One of the legends about Tadodaho described him as an evil monster with live snakes in his hair and seven crooks in his huge, twisted body.

Another legend describes his epic battle with a fellow Onondaga chief — Hai:watha, the Peacemaker's disciple. Because Hai:watha was preaching peace, Tadodaho came to regard him as a threat, so he set about to drive him away. In one version of the legend, Tadodaho killed Hai:watha's oldest daughter through witchcraft and defeated the relative who sought to kill him in revenge. Hai:watha wandered aimlessly for days, blind with grief. One day he came to a lake and found many white and colored shells along the shore. From them he made three strings of wampum. Hai:watha composed three speeches to mark his grief and used the wampum strings to rehearse his speeches after he made camp each night.

When Hai:watha reached the land of the Mohawk, he met another man of peace, Deganawida, the Peacemaker, who gave him more wampum strings in sympathy for his sorrow. (This was the origin of the Condolence Ceremony.) Relieved from his sorrow, Hai:watha set out with renewed vigor to help the Peacemaker and to isolate Tadodaho by converting all the rest of the Five Nations to their peace plan.

Finally, Hai:watha and the Peacemaker encountered Tadodaho. The evil war chief probably thought they meant to take revenge on him. Instead, they sat down with him and told him the details of their proposed Confederacy of Five Nations. As they described their plan, Tadodaho became more and more pleased. Far from taking away what little power he had left, this plan would make his people, the Onondaga, the Keepers of the Central Fire, and he, himself, would be the one to cast the deciding vote in any dispute in the Council of the Five Nations. Instead of becoming an old, embittered former war chief, he could see himself becoming a respected *raianer* in the Confederacy, with a chance to redeem himself for his past sins. Good, in the form of Hai:watha, Jigonsaseh, and the Peacemaker, had triumphed over evil, in the form of Tadodaho.

The once lawless warlord Tadodaho did what he had vowed never to do. He firmly embraced the Great Law of Peace. Hia:watha (which means "He Who Combs") had combed the snakes of evil out of Tadodaho's hair. And Tadodaho lit the fire for the first Grand Council.

THE EFFECTS OF THE AMERICAN REVOLUTION
ON THE SIX NATIONS CONFEDERACY

For centuries the Five Nations were at peace with each other. However, the Seneca still guarded the Western Door and the Mohawk still defended the Eastern Door. In the 1600s, when the French invaded the Great Longhouse, the Iroquois were outraged and almost destroyed the French colonies in retaliation over the next few years.

About two centuries later, the American colonists declared war on Britain. Because the Confederacy had been created to make it easier to practice peace than war, the decision as to whether to fight on the side of the British or the Americans was easy. If no consensus could be reached, then no action was to be taken. Joseph Thayendenegea Brant, the Mohawk Pine Tree chief, found out how difficult it was to obtain a consensus to fight on the side of the British. Although not a *raianer*, he had a special position because he was a Pine Tree chief, one who had special talent or skills which were of use to his nation. Sir William Johnson, superintendent of Indian affairs in the American colonies, had married Joseph Brant's older sister, Molly. After Sir

William's death, his son-in-law, Colonel Guy Johnson, was appointed superintendent of Indian affairs, and Joseph Brant agreed to become his secretary. Soon afterwards, he also became war chief of the Six Nations. In spite of all these honors, Thayendenegea was still unable to persuade all Six Nations to fight on the British side.

This failure to come to a consensus meant that each nation decided what to do on its own. The Elder Brothers, the Mohawk and the Seneca, supported the British, with whom they had longstanding trading agreements. Two of the Younger Brothers, the Oneida and the Tuscarora, decided to join the Americans, and the Onondaga and the Cayuga spoke for neutrality. This lack of consensus hurt the Confederacy, although it did not destroy it completely.

After the Americans won the war, they confiscated most of the Six Nations Territory, even though many had remained neutral or had actively fought on the Rebel side. However, the British had promised at the start of the war to replace any land lost by the Six Nations — in return for their military support. After negotiations by the Six Nations — and particularly by Thayendenegea — Governor Frederick Haldimand granted the Six Nations, by proclamation, six miles on either side of the Grand River from its source to its mouth. This tract of land was about a tenth the amount of land the Confederacy had had in what was now the United States.

In 1784 Joseph Brant led the first group of Six Nations to a landing which eventually became known as Brant's Ford, where the city of Brantford is now situated. The settlement began as a Mohawk village. Other villages then sprang up, farther down the river. The Onondaga nation's village and council house were situated where the hamlet of Middleport now stands, and the Tuscarora village was two or three miles upstream. The Cayuga and Seneca settlements were downstream.

During the war, many other First Nations had joined Thayendenegea. These people also came to the tract of land on the Grand River: the Siouian-speaking Tutelo (probably from the West); the Algonkian-speaking Nanticoke; and the Delaware, or Lenni-Lenapé (the "grandfathers" of the Algonkian-speaking people, who had been poised to become the seventh nation when the American Revolution began).

RECONSTITUTING THE CONFEDERACY

Soon after their arrival in 1784, the Six Nations Confederacy was restored as the traditional government. Some clan mothers and Confederacy *raianer* were among the people who came to the Grand River; others had died or had chosen to stay on the U.S. side of the border. The clans who were without representation chose new clan mothers, who each selected a new candidate to be condoled, or appointed, as *raianer*.

It is an exaggeration to say that the American Revolution caused the death of the Six Nations Confederacy. The Confederacy survived as the governing body at the Grand River Tract for 140 years, until 1924, when the Canadian government refused to deal with the Confederacy Council and installed an elected, municipal style of government. Barring the Confederacy Council from using the council house did not destroy it, however. The council just moved to one of the Onondaga longhouses. So the Confederacy still lives on, and many supporters boycott the elections of the government-backed band council.

In later years, the Confederacy showed it still had clout. In 1930, it sent a delegation of nine people to England, traveling with passports issued by the Confederacy itself, complete with its own seal. The delegation made a presentation to the British House of Commons and discussed the Haldimand Deed, through which the territory at Six Nations was formally deeded to the Six

Nations in recognition of their role as allies of the British Crown during the American Revolution. They also spoke about the Two-Row Wampum Treaty and the Covenant Chain of Friendship — an agreement of peaceful coexistence made in 1677 between the English colonies and the Native people of the eastern U.S. (led by the Iroquois).

In 1942, during World War II, the Six Nations Band Council gave the Canadian Department of National Defence permission to build an airport on land at the west end of the Six Nations Territory. The Confederacy *raianer* were not in agreement, however. Their thinking was that Canada had so much land that it did not need any part of the Six Nations' small territory for an airport. They also knew that prospects of the land being returned to the Six Nations after the war were not good.

The Confederacy *raianer* directed their secretary to write directly to His Majesty King George VI of Britain, informing him of their opposition to the confiscation of the land. The Department of National Defence had already started bulldozing some buildings and fences when a favorable reply came from Britain. *Raianer* James Squire Hill took the letter to the army barracks and read the statement from His Majesty, the King. The army workers moved their machinery off the Six Nations land at once.

These are two examples of the influence and prestige the Six Nations Confederacy still had, years after having been officially replaced by the elected band council.

THE SENECA PROPHET HANDSOME LAKE

Handsome Lake was a Seneca chief and architect of a great revival movement to address issues of the survival of Haudenosaunee society. In the face of social upheaval resulting from European encroachment on the Iroquois territories, the revival began in 1799, with Handsome Lake's first instructions, and continued throughout the following sixteen years. During this time, he preached the *Gaiwiio* (Guy-wee-yo) — "the Good Message," words from the Creator — to deal with the social disorder resulting from the European presence. His story and instructions are now referred to as the moral Code of Handsome Lake. In Cayuga, Handsome Lake's name is Skaniyadio, and in

Mohawk, it is Skanniatariio. Both names translate as "a beautiful lake" — a chief's title belonging to the Seneca nation.

In his younger days, during the American Revolution, Handsome Lake had been one of the many Six Nations chiefs who joined Joseph Thayendenegea Brant's army in their raids against the Americans. By the time he was middle aged, however, he had become an alcohol abuser. Like many alcoholics, he could feel himself declining and was repentant but was unable to help himself — and all around him he saw other men, and women, of the Seneca nation in a similar situation.

When Handsome Lake received his first set of instructions, he heard his name being called, and on reaching the door of his home, he saw three men dressed in traditional finery, with feathered bonnets on their heads. These Three Messengers had been sent by the Creator to help Handsome Lake recover because he had truly displayed remorse for his sins. They told him where to find some healing herbal medicine and charged him to deliver the Good Message from the Creator. They also told him to expect a Fourth Messenger at a later time.

Then the broken man collapsed. When his daughter and her husband found him, they thought he was dead, so they laid him in his bed and called Handsome Lake's brother Cornplanter and his nephew Wirecutter. No heartbeat could be detected, but when Wirecutter and some neighbors carried his body into the house to prepare him for burial, they found a warm spot on his chest. The warm spot began to grow, and by noon, Handsome Lake had regained consciousness and immediately began to describe the instructions to his family.

The Three Messengers are sometimes referred to as Three Angels. The First Good Message, or Set of Instructions, they brought was sent by the Creator to put a stop to four evils that the Six Nations people were practicing. It followed, they said, that the Good Message would restore happiness and peace of mind in Iroquois society.

The first evil was *ohnéga* (alcohol). Before the arrival of the white traders, alcohol and liquor were not available to the Longhouse People, and, therefore, they did not present a social problem. It was understood that the Europeans (the Younger Brothers of the Iroquois) consumed alcohol and liquor as a type of medicine, to be taken in moderation. Some Younger Brothers consumed alcohol or liquor in the morning, at noon, and in the evening, when their work was done. But the Longhouse People began to abuse this medicine, resulting in a social problem. So, as its use spread, it became necessary for someone in the traditional religious community to recognize this new threat to Iroquois society.

The three other evil practices were *góhtgoh* (witchcraft), *onohweht* (love medicine), and *godadwiyadoh:doh* (she cuts off birth) — medicine to prevent conception. These three evils made the Creator sad because they interfered with His plan. It is said that the Creator gives every person a certain number of days to rest on Mother Earth, and people are not supposed to make a mockery of Creation by cutting life short or by not fulfilling the number days given by the Creator. These evils, then, were thought to prevent one from enjoying social, mental, nutritional, physical, and spiritual well-being.

Handsome Lake asked his brother Cornplanter to call the people together in council and tell them the Good Message. (He was still too ill to make the announcement himself.) At the time of the council, Henry Simmons and Joel Swayne, two Quakers who were building a schoolhouse nearby, came at Cornplanter's request and heard the story through an interpreter. Simmons made a record of Handsome Lake's vision in his diary. The account moved everyone greatly and even the Quaker Simmons had good things to say about Handsome Lake's experience, although his beliefs were different.

Several weeks after the first instructions, the predicted Fourth Messenger did arrive. He appeared like the Creator in a dream. The next day, Handsome Lake fell into a trance for several hours and received his second set of instructions. The first Three Messengers were there when the Fourth Messenger joined them, and like the others, he was "wearing sky-blue clothes and carrying a bow and arrow." The Fourth Messenger then led him on a Sky Journey, where he viewed the Creator's Heaven. The Fourth Messenger also revealed to Handsome Lake the moral plan of all

Creation, which became the *Gaiwiio*, or moral Code of Handsome Lake.

One part of the long vision showed Handsome Lake three groups of people. The first group was large, the second was middle-sized, and the third was small. The large group were the ones who had not repented, the middle group were the half-hearted believers, and the small group were the true believers in the *Gaiwiio*. In another part of his vision, he and his guide traveled up to a fork in the Great Sky Road and followed the Narrow Road toward where the Creator lived. Along this road were beautiful birds, the sweet scent of flowers, and delicious fruits, including strawberries.

Handsome Lake, Cornplanter, and Wirecutter were among the first adherents to the moral Code of Handsome Lake. The Longhouse People, from this time forward, continued all the former ceremonies and now added the recitation of the *Gaiwiio* to the annual cycle of observances. To most people, the required changes made sense, but some of the more conservative followers of the old ways did not welcome them. Nevertheless, with the return of his health, Handsome Lake began to preach in earnest about the Good Message the Four Messengers had given him. He understood that the Creator had sent him back from near death and had given him these instructions for the people. Given this revival, Handsome Lake would eventually be referred to as a prophet.

GAIWIIO (THE GOOD MESSAGE)

The Good Message as first presented had two main themes. The first was a prophecy of impending disaster if the people continued on the path they were currently following. Plagues and crop failures would bring famine to the Seneca, and in the end, the earth would burn and all the wicked people would perish with it. The second theme was this: only those who refused to repent and show remorse would suffer and perish. But those who died without repenting would follow the wide path to the House of the Punisher — the evil brother of the Creator.

To Handsome Lake, it went without saying that the historical ceremonies would continue as before. Handsome Lake did not consider the Good Message to be a new religion. Instead, he believed he was restoring the morals and ethics of the Longhouse people in relation to European encroachment on the society of the day — so Iroquoian society could reinvent itself and survive into the future. Because he believed this, he felt secure in condemning certain practices.

For instance, Handsome Lake condemned four dances that required dancers to become partly or completely entranced or that had sexual connotations. (He had seen a vision of many canoes loaded with alcohol and a man jumping from one canoe to the other, singing *Gajiháya*, the song of the evil-minded spirit — and he realized the dancer was the Punisher himself, in human form. So he condemned the Devil's Dance (*Gajiháya*) and three other favorite dances of the Evil Spirit.)

Handsome Lake also reminded his people of the four great ceremonies which are now celebrated as the Thanksgiving Ceremonies: the Great Feather Dance (*Ostowahgo:wa*); the Drum Dance (*Ganèho:*), to give thanks and to honor the Four Messengers; the Personal Male Songs (*Adó:wa*); and the Great Dish Game (*Gayedowá:neh*). An adjunct to the *Adó:wa* is the Naming Ceremony, in which the speaker announces the clan names of the parents of the child being named. The speaker or his designate then speaks on behalf of the father and mentions the child's new name. Then a song, or *Adó:wa* (prayer of thanksgiving to the Creator), is rendered while the child walks with, or is carried by, the speaker.

These ceremonies of thanksgiving are said to have been delivered by a "Fatherless Boy" — and they existed prior to the moral Code of Handsome Lake.* The story of the Fatherless Boy goes this way.

THE FATHERLESS BOY

In ancient times, twelve male babies were born in a Native village. Eleven of them had fathers, but one had been born of a virgin mother and became known as the Fatherless Boy. Almost at once, unusual events happened in connection with him. When the eleven mothers felt well enough after

*This version of the Story of the Fatherless Boy was told by Deskaheh (Alexander J. General), a condoled *raianer* of the Cayuga Young Bear Clan. The account is recorded in Frank G. Speck's *Midwinter Rites of the Cayuga Long House* (Lincoln, Nebraska: University of Nebraska Press, 1977). Speck, an anthropologist from the University of Pennsylvania, attended seven days of the Midwinter Ceremonies in 1933 and 1936 and parts of the ceremony in 1934, 1935, 1944, and 1945.

their deliveries, each of them set out separately to visit the mother of the Fatherless Boy. To their surprise, they all arrived at the same time — as if their visits had been planned. As time passed, this happened again and again.

One day when they were visiting, the eleven mothers noticed that the Fatherless Boy was teaching their sons three ceremonies: the Great Feather Dance (*Ostowahgo:wa*), the Drum Dance (*Ganèho:*), and the Personal Male Songs (*Adó:wa*). When the Fatherless Boy asked for someone to volunteer to practice the *Adó:wa*, one boy tried and found he could perform it as if he had been

doing it for years — because he had the help of the Fatherless Boy. This child and the other ten grew up and carried on these sacred ceremonies.

After they were all grown, the eleven friends and the Fatherless Boy met again one day at the usual place. The Fatherless Boy told them he had to travel to a country in the East, across the salt water, to teach the people there. He walked away down a trail and disappeared from their sight behind a large pine tree.

Years later, one of the eleven, now old and grey, went to visit the spot where they used to play. To his surprise, he found his ten friends there at the same time. Then, coming toward them up the trail from the east came the Fatherless Boy, now grown. They pressed forward, happy to greet him once more, but he warned them not to try to shake his hand or touch him. He told them, "They would not accept my words. Instead, they punished me and tried to put me to death." He showed them his bloodied hands and feet, and he said they had been pierced by metal. "But I have come back," he said, "to teach you the Great Dish Game before I return to the land of the Creator." Then the Fatherless Boy took out some peach pits and a bowl and proceeded to teach the game. As they were playing and learning the rules, the Fatherless Boy disappeared, and it is assumed that he continued his journey to the Creator.

The Fatherless Boy, in some circles, is considered to be the son of the Creator.

IROQUOIS PERFORMERS AND ARTISTS

Handsome Lake reminded his people of the ceremonies — the dances and the ceremonial game — that had been theirs in the past but had been neglected. Today, these ceremonies are still held by the followers of the Longhouse but they are not presented for public entertainment, since they are sacred and to be held in reverence.

The social dances and the pow-wow dances, however, are performed for the general public and for entertainment — and many dance performers are featured in this book. They are part of a tradition of Iroquoian artists, performers, and competitive athletes who have risen to prominence over the years.

For instance, a hundred years ago, Pauline Johnson toured Canada, reciting her own poetry about Aboriginal people. Her childhood home, Chiefswood, is now a museum on the Six Nations Territory, near Brantford, Ontario. *Flint and Feather,* an edition combining two of her books of poetry, has recently been reprinted.

In 1907 Tom Longboat, another man from Six Nations, won the Boston Marathon and went on to beat the best professionals in the world — to say nothing of the horse he bested in a twelve-mile race between the villages of Hagersville and Caledonia on the Grand River. He was named the top runner in Canada for the half-century between 1900 and 1950, and in more recent years, the Tom Longboat Trophy has been awarded periodically to outstanding Native athletes in Canada.

During the Great Depression of the 1930s, outstanding Iroquois lacrosse players left Ontario, Quebec, and New York State for British Columbia to try their luck at professional lacrosse. One of those young men — Harry Smith — headed south to California after the lacrosse season was over. Smith's speed and athletic ability impressed actor Joe E. Brown, and he helped him get started in Hollywood. Taking the stage name Jay Silverheels, Smith appeared as a supporting actor in many movies before landing the starring role of Tonto on *The Lone Ranger*. He also appeared as Tonto in the *Lone Ranger* movie. Sometimes the script called for a few Native words. Whether he was supposed to be an Apache or a Commanche, he usually said something in Mohawk, much to the delight of his friends back home. This was an "in" joke, which only fluent Mohawk speakers could enjoy.

Thirty years later, Graham Greene, an Oneida from Six Nations, learned to speak his lines in Lakota for the film *Dances with Wolves*. His portrayal of the Lakota medicine man Kicking Bird earned him a 1990 Academy Award nomination for Best Supporting Actor. Like Jay Silverheels before him, he practiced his craft for over a dozen years before becoming a well-known actor. In the 1980s, Greene was cast in a number of plays in London, England, and appeared regularly on two TV series, *Spirit Bay* and *Nine B.* In 1989, he appeared in an award-winning play, *Dry Lips Oughta Move to Kapuskasing,* by Tomson Highway — for which he won a Dora Mavor Moore Award for his role as Pierre St. Pierre. He has played French and English military officers, a seventy-year-old Jewish man, and the ghost of a black transvestite. It would not be surprising to see him playing Shakespeare's Macbeth in the future.

Gary Dale Farmer, a Cayuga of the Wolf Clan, was also born on the Six Nations Territory and has extensive experience in movies, television, theatre, and radio. In 1989 he played a major role in Thomson Highway's *Dry Lips* and also took on a leading role in the film *Powwow Highway.* More recently, he has starred in *Smoke Signals,* a feature-length movie about life on a U.S. reservation, and directed a National Film Board documentary, *The Gift* — the story of corn and its economic, political, traditional, and spiritual importance in North America. He is also editor-in-chief of the magazine *Aboriginal Voices.*

In ancient times, music and dancing were a part of the Iroquois's everyday lifestyle. But the modern descendants of these people have branched out from drums and rattles to guitars, keyboards, and other instruments. They have also embraced a wide variety of music styles, including country and western, rock and roll, blue grass, and blues.

One of these young people was a child prodigy. In 1958, at the age of fourteen, Robbie Robertson was already a veteran of several bands. His mother had taken him with her to a Toronto suburb, but as a boy at Six Nations, he had heard lots of country music and blues. When he came back for visits to his uncle's house, he saw his cousin Herb Mike and his friends picking and singing. At a young age he decided he was going to play music all over the world.

So when Rompin' Ronnie Hawkins let Robbie join his band, he became one of the Hawks who barnstormed across southern Ontario and the United States for five years. The Hawks left Ronnie Hawkins in 1963 when Robbie was only nineteen. But he was already a seasoned veteran, so when the Hawks joined Bob Dylan and became The Band, Robbie did most of the writing and composing for "Up on Cripple Creek" and "The Night They Drove Old Dixie Down."

After Dylan was forced to stop touring because of a motorcycle accident, he and The Band had time to do more recordings. The Band moved into a big pink house near Dylan's home in Woodstock, New York, and their first release, *Music from Big Pink,* received rave reviews. In 1969, the famous Woodstock festival was the place to be and, of course, The Band was there.

One of Robbie Robertson's songs, "The Weight," was later recorded by Aretha Franklin, The Supremes, and The Temptations — and The Band produced five more studio albums, with songs like "The Shape I'm In," "Life Is a Carnival," and "Acadian Driftwood." The Band's final concert was made into a film directed by Martin Scorsese called *The Last Waltz.* After it was released in 1978, Robbie was offered a major part in the movie *Carny.* The film failed at the box office, but Robbie went on to produce music for the films *Raging Bull, The King of Comedy,* and *The Color of Money.*

But it is one of his latest albums, *Contact from the Underworld of Red Boy,* that has brought him back to his roots, the traditions of the Longhouse people. In his travels, he had met many other First Nations musicians, and he saw this album and a previous one — *Music for the Native Americans* — as a way to bring the evolving Native music he had encountered to the attention of a wider audience.

From the legends of Creation to modern-day music heros, the story of the Iroquois, like that of so many other nations, has been fraught with upheaval and invention. In the pages that follow, you will meet men and women of all ages and many, varied gifts: dancers, artists, high-steel construction workers, teachers, lawyers, grandmothers, grandfathers, faithkeepers, and *raianer.* They are all dancers in their own right. We invite you to join their dance and journey for the next few hours.

THE PEOPLE

"Jesus Christ loves you!"

"He gives strength to the weary and increases the power of the weak."
ISAIAH 40:29 (NIV)

You don't stand a chance against my prayers
You don't stand a chance against my love . . .
But we shall live again, we shall live again

— ROBBIE ROBERTSON

PETER SKY ～ Peter Sky's mother was a faithkeeper at the Onondaga Longhouse on the
Six Nations Territory. His father was a faithkeeper at the Cayuga Longhouse. As a family, the Skys went
to the Seneca Longhouse, in deference to parents who were buried there. And when Peter's name was

put forth for chief, the clan mothers decided he should go to
the Onondaga Longhouse, where his mother was faithkeeper,
and be chief there.

He grew up on the family farm, tending to cows and pigs,
alongside his father and grandfather, and speaking a steady
stream of Cayuga to the two men as they completed their
chores. Then, when he spoke to his mother, he used her
language, Onondaga. As a result, he emerged from his
childhood fully fluent in both languages.

Peter is a firekeeper for the Onondaga Longhouse. He
opens the Council meetings, which are held on the first
Saturday of every month. At these meetings, the Confederacy
business is conducted as it has always been. Peter explains,
"The Longhouse people percentage is really small. But we
still do what we have to do. And decision making in the
Confederacy is still done."

Peter met his wife, a faithkeeper herself, at the Cayuga
Longhouse. They have six children and many grandchildren who live close at hand on the Six Nations
Territory. One grandson plays lacrosse in British Columbia.

Peter, an Ondondaga of the Deer Clan, is named Hojekhteih, which means "Shouldering
Encouragements."

nerosity has helped transform

PAMELA BOMBERRY ~ Of all the women in the Bomberry family, Pamela is

unique. She loves team sports — basketball, volleyball, and especially lacrosse. In the early evenings of late spring, Pamela, with other members of the Six Nations Girls Field Lacrosse team, hones her skills and practices the plays that will make them serious contenders in league games. To people on the Six Nations Territory, with whom lacrosse is unrivaled in popularity, Pamela and her team truly are the girls of summer.

Social dancing is an intrinsic part of traditional Longhouse life. Some, like Pamela, who dances with Jim Sky's group, go on to present the dances to audiences at large, in a manner of exposition. Following in the footsteps of her three older sisters, and no doubt encouraged by her grandmother, Pamela learned western-style pow-wow dancing, competing as a jingle-dress dancer at first and later as a traditional dancer. She dances only occasionally now, preferring the competition in the field to that in the circle.

Pamela's mother is Mohawk of the Turtle Clan. Pamela's name is Gawadsidsawi — one that resides with the Turtle Clan. It means "She Is Picking Flowers."

ROBERT JACOB HILL ～ At the age of ten, Robert Hill left his home on the

Six Nations Territory and moved with his parents to North Carolina. He started a new school and made a few friends. He saw his family — his grandfather, Jim Sky, and his cousins, aunts, and uncles — when they came to North Carolina to present the traditional social dances of the Iroquois. In fact, he joined them. He knew every dance.

In summers, Robert came home. He returned to his grandfather, to familiar fields and footpaths and places to play — and to the game that stands on its own above all others, lacrosse. Four summers came and went in this way. On the fifth summer, he asked to stay.

He started a new school with old friends. He returned to the Longhouse and the familiar phrases of the Cayuga language and to the place where he is once again known as Dihoh. What he always understood after he had left home was that home had never left him.

Robert is a Cayuga of the Bear Clan. He is named Had ya Dihoh, which means "Something in the Sky."

COLLIN ANDREW ROY HALL ~

(LEFT) This young man has many names but answers to none of them. He answers to Joe. That's his nickname.

Joe is at the doorstep of high school and his first school experience off reserve. Akwesasne Mohawk School, situated on Cornwall Island, has prepared him in science and mathematics and other fundamentals of a primary school education, and, more — it has given him a profound sense of his own identity. He has learned to read and write in his own language and received cultural teachings that complement his Longhouse knowledge and the traditional values espoused by his parents and grandparents.

Joe spends his summers working with his father, learning to net lacrosse sticks. As the Mohawk International Lacrosse league supplies more teams, Joe's summer employment is pretty well assured. It may be the career he chooses.

Joe, of many names, has one more name. It belongs to him and in his lifetime, no one else will have it. That name is Shate'Karonhi:io. It means "Middle of the Sky." On the day of his photograph, Shate'Karonhi:io wore his father's headdress. It was a proud day.

MACKENZIE MITCHELL ~

(RIGHT) Mackenzie Mitchell has a very old Mohawk name. His grandfather, Richard Mitchell, wanted Mack to have the name of his own great-grandfather. So Mack is named Kariwatiron. Unlike most Mohawk names, it cannot be translated. It is a name that stands on its own.

The Midwinter Ceremonies take place in January and occur over a period of eight days for the purpose of giving thanks for the blessings of life, health, and community. Mack goes every day. In the spring, when the sap is running, he dresses in his traditional Iroquois clothes, buckskin leggings, breechcloth, ribbon shirt, and the traditional headdress — the *kastówah* — and goes to the Maple Syrup Ceremony, to give thanks that there will be maple syrup for another year.

Throughout the year, there will be other rites of thanksgiving and of appeal, and Mack will be at all of them. For now, because he is just seven, he sits and tries to understand and prepare for a future when he may be chosen to lead the Mohawks of Akwesasne in song and dance and expressions of thanks.

CLAYTON LOGAN ~

Clayton Logan delivered the opening prayer at the Grand River Pow-Wow on the Six Nations Territory. He spoke in the Seneca language with a fluency that belied an exile of twenty-four years from his community at Cattaraugus. To those who marvel at this, he explains, "I did my prayers in my language, in the manner that I knew, to communicate with our Creator and pretty much kept up with things. I knew when the ceremonies took place and would make it a point to try and get back home for them."

A military career in the United States Navy took him to distant locations throughout the United States and beyond, including a tour of duty in Vietnam. In 1970, he chose a posting in Spain and planned to

later retire in Florida, but when he saw he was needed as a speaker in his own community, he returned to Cattaraugus.

A man of many surprises, Clayton played the role of Chief Bromden in a stage production of *One Flew Over the Cuckoo's Nest* in Salamanca, New York, and he can be heard as the voice of Elie S. Parker in a documentary about the condoled sachem who became an engineer and U.S. brigadier-general.

Veterans have an honored place at pow-wows and Clayton is frequently invited to carry the American flag. When the flag is retired, he dances. And he is easy to pick out in a crowd. He's a grass dancer. In a circle filled with young men engaged in a dance so demanding of stamina and athleticism, he is there, body bending and bowing in smooth and fluid movements. An ageless man in a timeless dance.

It is often the case that names given to infants may be replaced at adulthood. Clayton's name, Jo On Dod, was set aside for him before his birth, and it is a name the clan mother declared should stay with him for his lifetime. Jo On Dod, a Seneca name of the Wolf Clan, means "Tree Standing."

BOB JAMIESON ~ At the age of two, Bob Jamieson was placed in a foster home on the Six Nations Territory. He got as far as Grade Eight in school. In his teen years, he went to work as a hired hand on a farm, and on one of his birthdays, a young girl about Bob's age from the neighboring farm baked a cake for him. It was the first time his birthday had ever been celebrated. He was so moved that he took to courting her. They married, and he began farming his own land.

Bob Jamieson remained committed to the "Indian question," a phrase used to describe active probes into the status of land claims and remembrance of the history of how the Iroquois arrived at the Grand River and held its territory. With fluency in four Iroquoian languages and an understanding of the remaining two, he was well positioned to serve as official interpreter for the elders and condoled chiefs. He was included in presentations in Ottawa to two governors general and in New York to a United Nations subcommittee.

A seasoned orator, Bob spoke every year at the Border Crossing Ceremonies at Fort Erie. He was active in the Longhouse ceremonies as a speaker, and took his family with him. On Sundays, he went to service at the United Church.

Bob Jamieson passed away at the age of eighty.

Beating hearts, beating hearts
Come as one, come as one
This is Indian country
This is Indian country

— ROBBIE ROBERTSON

LORI SKY MARTIN ～ Lori Sky Martin spent many hours of her childhood as a groom and many more in the saddle, gaining expertise to compete in the flag- and barrel-racing events of western horse shows.

Along with her father and other family members, she presented the traditional social dances of the Iroquois in venues throughout Ontario and in the eastern United States.

Lori Sky teaches at the Emily C. General School on the Six Nations Territory. The route she took to prepare for a teaching career was, of necessity, long and arduous; it took seven years. With a son to raise, she chose to balance her time between earning and learning, concentrating initially on a teaching assistant certificate and then on a Bachelor of Education degree from Queen's University. Now she has taken her place as a true caretaker of the Cayuga language, guiding it to a place of understanding within the minds of her students, preserving it and ensuring its future as a vital link to all that has gone before.

Lori, a Cayuga of the Bear Clan, chose the name Guywahnonh. It means '"Guarding the Way." In a way, that is what she is doing.

MICHEAL BOMBERRY ~

Before Micheal Bomberry could walk on his own, his mother took his hand and led him to the circle amidst a great gathering of people. As the sounds began, of the drum and the voices raised in song, she led Micheal in a clockwise direction, and together they danced in a pow-wow. He watched his uncles execute the intricately subtle gestures of the traditional

men's dance and he learned. He listened to the songs and commenced a tentative re-enactment of what he saw, and he brought to his practice a depth of focus and a curiosity that looked for the moment of truth in every movement.

But it is the counterclockwise dances of the Longhouse that give Micheal his most potent connection to dance, a form of expression that is innately his, bred in the bone, like an ancient memory waiting to be recalled. To hear him speak about the Longhouse ceremonies, one is struck by the depth of understanding that springs from a mind that is still so young — and it sparks some speculation about the role he may have in the years that lie ahead. Responding to this, Micheal said, "You can't say that you want to be a faithkeeper or anything. It is how you carry yourself within the Longhouse and wherever you are. And the people see that you have a good mind and a good heart. That's how you are chosen."

There is a group of men and women at Six Nations, known collectively as Ojihgwagayohn, who gather regularly to sing. In late fall, they meet more frequently, three or four times a week, to prepare for Sing, an annual gathering of singers from all of the Iroquoian reserves who meet in a different place each year and bring their songs to sing for each other. Micheal will be there. He may even have a song of his own to sing, a new song that will have found its way from an ancient chord.

Micheal, a Mohawk of the Turtle Clan, is named Oh no:do. It means "Flood."

LEIGH SMITH ~ A Mohawk who came to live at Six Nations when she was eight years old, Leigh Smith enjoyed a childhood filled with culture — with the songs, dances, orations, and ceremonies of the Longhouse.

She had within her a curiosity about the world. After graduating from high school, she joined the North American Indian Travelling College, and with a group of students, elders, and others from various Iroquois reserves, Leigh went west. She visited Indian territories in the American Midwest and traded histories with the people she met.

She found her life's work when she married Steven Smith, a fledgling potter and the son of famed Iroquois potter Elda Smith. Encouraged by Elda, Leigh learned the art of creating traditional Iroquois pottery using modern techniques. Within a few years, Leigh and Steven opened their own pottery studio on Six Nations. They called it Talking Earth Pottery and began experimenting with new colors and designs, resulting in a new style made from the marriage of old and new.

Leigh Smith talks with her hands. She speaks volumes.

Leigh, a Mohawk of the Turtle Clan, received the name Goh was son noh gwas. It means "Picking Names from the Water."

STEVEN SMITH ~

Steven Smith was given the name Karon Hia Te, which means "Standing Sky." He is the son of Oliver and Elda Smith, who brought their unique and differing strengths to the preservation of Iroquois culture, in its language and history, and in its arts and crafts. They are a part of modern-day Iroquois history.

Like so many Mohawk men before him, Steven Smith graduated from high school and went to work in the high-steel industry — but a fortuitous strike by the union sent Steven home. There he rekindled his interest in pottery, and under the guidance of his mother, Elda, began to experiment with a variety of clays and with different decorating and firing techniques. He created his own method of smoke-firing pieces and produced traditional works with an ancient appearance. He experimented further, and combining his love of Japanese raku pottery and Iroquois pottery, he created new pieces shaped from both cultures.

Through their Talking Earth Pottery studio, Steven and his wife, Leigh, have carved a niche for themselves in the potters' world at large — with their pieces so full of promises and ancient memories. The digging continues. The earth talks. And Standing Sky has his ear to the ground, listening.

JACK MOORE ～

Jack Moore is a Pima and Pueblo man who traveled north looking for a place to call home. He found it in the heart of a young Oneida woman who took him as her husband. With that, Jack was welcomed into a sprawling Iroquois family and accepted as a brother. That was in 1982.

He is the father of three high-spirited and highly individual Oneida boys who dance alongside their father in pow-wows throughout the summer. They started young: they were babies when they first heard the music Jack played for them. He and his wife, Rhonda, put their hands together and made traditional

outfits for each one of them. The boys watched Jack as he feathered the bustles they would wear. In this way, they each learned the patient art of creating their regalia.

For Jack, dancing for recognition and prizes came a few years after he had set his first foot inside the pow-wow circle. At first, it was a way of connecting, of joining kin and kindred spirits, and of being at one with a multitude who listened with one ear. He danced at every opportunity, improving his skill and understanding of the traditional dance, and then he entered competition. In time, Jack became a prize-winning dancer.

Jack was a boy himself, in his teens, and not much older than his eldest son, Cody, when he ventured out on his own. He arrived in Windsor rather circuitously, traveling by way of New York City, and liked it immediately. To Jack, it was a quiet little city with work. It was a place where he could touch down for a spell. He didn't know then that Windsor was the place that would claim him. He found work. He found belonging. And he found fulfillment.

Jack Moore's name resides with the Eagle Clan. He is called Kord Da Sek, which means "Doing Things Backwards."

Everyone has a song / God gave us each a song
That's how we know who we are / Everyone has a song

— ROBBIE ROBERTSON

FRANCIS FROMAN ~

Francis Froman is a clan mother, one in a long line of women whose lives were filled with an important purpose: to preserve the language and culture of their people. She teaches Cayuga to children at I.L. Thomas School on the Six Nations Territory.

As a clan mother, she participates in the Naming Ceremony at the Midwinter Ceremonies, and she will assume a role in the Stirring Ashes Ceremony, which is held on the first two days of the Midwinter Ceremonies. She will assist in preparing the foods — the corn soup, the bread, and the berry juice that will be served at the conclusion of the third day of the rites.

Francis has seven daughters and a son, and they, in their turn, have sons and daughters who by now have sons and daughters of their own. The traditions have been passed on. Pride in the culture lives on in each of them.

Francis is named Gah nish oha. It is a name that resides with the Wolf Clan, and it means "Covered with Sand."

TIA THOMPSON ~ It is a long time ago that Tia Thompson picked up a lacrosse

stick for the first time. She is so comfortable with it that it feels like an extension of herself, a personal fixture permanently attached to her. She plays on the senior lacrosse team for General Vanier Secondary School in Cornwall, Ontario. This past season, they took on a crack team of international players at Lake Placid and won.

Tia had her first taste of political activism this year when her school was slated for closure. With a sizable population of Mohawk students from Akwesasne, it offers Native and Mohawk language studies as credit courses. The students protested and won, for a while at least. The school will stay open for another year.

No one has had a more influential role in guiding and shaping Tia than her mother, Louise Thompson, who says, "We are Mohawks not because we have a band number but because we still have our dances and our ceremonies and our culture." These are Tia's birthrights.

A Mohawk of the Wolf Clan, Tia is named Wentenhawi, which means "Bringing in the Dawn."

STEVEN CHIP PARKER ~ You should see Chip Parker dance. He made his
first grand entry at the age of three. In his first competition pow-wow, he danced in the Tiny Tot division
and won, and he is still winning. Chip has also danced in Connecticut, and in recognition of his ability,
he was presented with an eagle feather. It is the old-style traditional dancing that Chip does, disciplined
by subtlety and nuance, and chock full of history. He dances in an outfit of the Sioux style.

The dances and the songs of the Longhouse ceremonies have been taught to Chip. His grandmother,
who is raising him, has ensured that he will have an understanding of his culture and tradition to serve
as a foundation for future learning. That is why he attends the Native American Program School in
Buffalo with a curriculum that includes culture teaching.

He is a member of the Buffalo Creek Dancers, who perform the traditional Iroquois social dances. The
group, organized by Chip's aunts, performs at schools and cultural gatherings.

This little boy of nine, who is a vision of timelessness in dance, frequently escapes to the present — to
play video games like Clone Wars. He brags that he can beat his uncle on all levels.

Chip is a Seneca of the Heron Clan.

We are the People of the Longhouse
We are the People that you couldn't break
We are the People of the Sacred Pipe
Who follow the Code of Handsome Lake

— ROBBIE ROBERTSON

JAKE THOMAS ～

It is barely possible to think about the Great Law of Peace without the late Jake Thomas. For nine days every September, he recited it in five Iroquois languages. Once or twice, he recited it in English, and in doing so, he brought home the Great Law to a multitude of Iroquois who had either forgotten their mother tongue or had never learned it. This was his gift to them.

Jake Thomas, a Cayuga from the Sandpiper Clan, was given the name Hadajihgren tha, meaning "Descending Cloud." It was chosen for him at birth. As a condoled hereditary chief who was elevated by

the clan, he received the hereditary name De yohonwe thon.

Within Jake Thomas dwelled the history of the Iroquois. He was the keeper of stories, of the Constitution, and he knew every nuance of traditional protocol. He held the knowledge of the wampum and was one of a handful of chiefs who could be called upon by other Iroquois communities to conduct a Condolence Ceremony.

A lifetime student who was, at heart, a tireless educator, Jake Thomas was a professor of Native studies at Trent University in Peterborough, Ontario, for fourteen years and lectured on Iroquois traditions and culture at other universities. In 1993, he founded the Jake Thomas Learning Centre and dedicated it to the preservation and revitalization of Iroquois culture and tradition.

He carved masks, condolence canes, ceremonial bowls, and clan spoons and made traditional baskets and wampum belts.

At the age of fifty-two, when his fourteen children were grown, he began to learn the Great Law. In 1972, Jake Thomas recited it for the first time, speaking in Mohawk.

Perhaps to explain what compelled him to teach and recite the Great Law every year as he did, Jake often remarked, "When I go, people won't say I took all my knowledge to the grave." He didn't. Jake Thomas died on August 17, 1998, at the age of seventy-five. He left us all a little wiser.

BEATRICE THOMAS ～ In the summers of the mid-forties, farm operators around Brantford sent trucks through the Six Nations Territory for day workers to pick crops. Young Beatrice Thomas, sixteen years old and recently let out from the Mohawk Institute Residential School, rode the truck every day to a job in the fields. In her spare time, she watched lacrosse. While she watched the game, one of the players watched her. In time, the fan and the player were united in a marriage that produced ten children. Beatrice is a grandmother to many — she stopped counting at thirty-two.

Beatrice descends from a long line of Longhouse followers. She too has always followed the tradition, despite a brief interruption during her years at the Mohawk Institute, and she serves as a faithkeeper at the Seneca Longhouse. Now seventy and beset by frail health, Beatrice has taken on a helper. "I just go there and do my duty. My daughter takes over while I sit and watch."

A Mohawk of the Turtle Clan, Beatrice is named Go wa dah se, which means "Throwing for Someone."

With her on the banks of the Grand River are members of the next two generations: Deneen Hill and her son Leroy Johnson. Deneen, a mother of eight and a strong advocate for the Iroquois languages and traditions, is named Wahsonti:io, which means "Pleasant Night." Leroy was only about three weeks old when this picture was taken. He is named Teharonhi:iaks, which means "He Goes across the Sky."

JORDY MITCHELL ∼
At three years of age, Jordy Mitchell, a Mohawk of the Snipe Clan at Akwesasne Reserve, can count among his experiences several visits to the Longhouse. Knowledge of the Longhouse is part of his pre-kindergarten education.

His grandmother and great-grandmother speak to Jordy in Mohawk, and he has acquired the language with ease. When he begins grade school, Jordy will go to a Mohawk Immersion Program, where he will continue his language studies and receive traditional teaching. He will learn the dances, the songs, and the speeches that are part of Longhouse life, and in time, he will gain an understanding of the meaning behind each.

For now, Jordy will learn to play the traditional sport he likes so much: lacrosse.

Jordy was given his name, Sago wenthe tha, by his grandmother. It means "He's a Leader." And it once belonged to a relative who passed on long ago. By carrying this name, Sago wenthe tha will carry the spirit of one who was loved and respected in his own time, into the new century.

PERRY WILLIAMS ~

The day was cold. It was the kind of cold that the memory keeps crisp. A crowd of people stood in the road up by the Onondaga Longhouse, where a welcoming fire was burning. A sound of men singing could be heard, though it was faint, as if coming from a great distance. The singing men came down the road toward the fire. They burned tobacco in it, then made their way into the Longhouse. "Chief" called out the roll call. Every now and then, the men, who had taken their places on the benches, would respond. This was the day Perry Williams would be named a hereditary chief. "I was sitting there for a real long time," he recalls. "It took a long time to accept me in that position because I was just a boy. In the end they did.

"My grandmother was a clan mother, and as soon as something came up that was involved with chiefs, I was taken there by my grandmother. I wasn't a kid anymore. I couldn't go out and play. I had to sit inside with the chiefs."

Thirty-five years have passed since the boy of eight became a chief, and Perry Williams has come into his manhood, in the gradual manner of all men. He is a husband, father, and provider, working in concert with his wife to guide his children — two sons and two daughters, all in their teens — as they make their way to adulthood. He is a welder by trade who has, by turns, worked as a trucker and a subcontractor in the siding business.

A few years ago, Perry was chosen to be a faithkeeper, to help his community sustain the traditional observances that are an intrinsic part of the ceremonies in the Longhouse calendar. Perry Williams is living his life as destined.

A member of the Wolf Clan, Perry is named Tonhogehnghugs. In the Onondaga language, this means "Coming through the Door."

53

COREY THOMAS ～ Corey Thomas leads a sporting life that knows two seasons:

winter, when he plays hockey, and summer, when he plays lacrosse. He began playing lacrosse at the age of four, and now, at eleven, he has developed enough skill to earn a place on the traveling team for the Akwesasne Nighthawks in the Pee-Wee division.

Corey is a child of the Longhouse. It is worthwhile to note that a Longhouse ceremony is not a spectator experience. Participation is not merely expected; it is necessary. A situation like this can wreak havoc with a boy who is shy, like Corey. Luckily, he has a grandfather, who is not shy, to help him overcome any reticence.

Mohawk is the language of the Longhouse at Akwesasne. Translation is provided, and the community looks to its elders and its children to assist the in-betweeners, so that everyone can have an appreciation of what is being said. Corey is studying Mohawk every day at school, and there is no doubt that one day he will be called upon to relay the words of the speakers to the people.

Corey is named Kaheroton, which means "Standing Corn." He is a member of the Bear Clan.

DELSUN MOORE ~ Delsun Moore was born bouncing to the beat. He was born
to parents who danced in competition at pow-wows. He was born into the rhythm of practice and
performance. And he was born to receive the eagle feather that was given to his parents to keep for him
as a welcoming gift.

Soon Delsun, wearing the traditional outfit his parents made, entered the circle and danced alongside
his father. Delsun learned well. In the summer of 1999, he won the top prize in young men's traditional
dancing at the Champion of Champions Pow-Wow at Six Nations.

There is no moderation in his love for lacrosse. He began playing with the Windsor Warlocks and
discovered that the game was really a lot harder than it looked. Skilful playing was a tricky proposition.
It needed the kind of perseverance that only passion could bring — and Delsun had it. He triumphed.
At the end of the season, he was cited as the most improved player on the team. Delsun's dream is to
play for the team at Six Nations. And his passion even extends to the lacrosse stick itself. He collects
them. And wherever he goes, so goes his lacrosse stick.

Delsun's middle name, given to him at birth, is Red Bird. He is Pima/Oneida of the Bear Clan.

OLIVER JACOBS ～

Oliver Jacobs is a hereditary chief, a condoled chief, chosen many years ago by clan mothers as successor to a council member who had passed on. No longer a young man, Oliver still travels regularly to Confederacy Council meetings that are held throughout the Iroquois territories.

In Iroquois tradition, no distinction holds between the spiritual and the secular. They work together in a seamless pattern of belief. It falls to men like Oliver to speak the speeches that convey the teachings

that shape the lives of the Iroquois and guide them in their daily lives. He is, therefore, present at the Longhouse ceremonies as they are held throughout the year. In the days and sometimes weeks that lead up to the ceremonies, Oliver cloisters himself for periods of personal reflection on their true spiritual meaning.

There is another side to Oliver Jacobs. He is a social man who enjoys gatherings, large and small. He worked to organize and promote the Grand River Pow-Wow, an event that brings thousands to the Six Nations Territory every summer. Over the years, he has participated as a traditional dancer, though he has never entered the circle as a competitor. He did it for the joy of the dance and the fellowship of so many of good mind who came together to celebrate the tangibles that unite them as First Peoples and to share the offerings that make each of them distinct among First Peoples.

Like so many who came of age in the late thirties and early forties of the twentieth century, Oliver set to work in jobs that demanded brawn and a certain stoicism. He worked in gypsum mines and laid pipelines to support his wife and family. For nourishment, they drew on Oliver's constant and unwavering faith.

Oliver Jacobs, an Onondaga of the Turtle Clan, is named Deywah ta Hohseh, which means "Cross Roads."

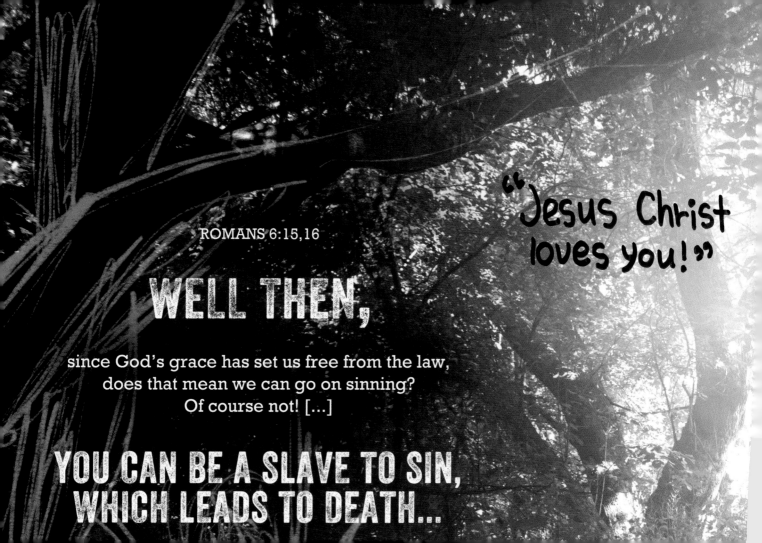

ROMANS 6:15,16

WELL THEN,

since God's grace has set us free from the law,
does that mean we can go on sinning?
Of course not! [...]

YOU CAN BE A SLAVE TO SIN,
WHICH LEADS TO DEATH...

"Jesus Christ loves you!"

SANTEE SMITH ~

Santee Smith is a Mohawk of the Turtle Clan from the Six Nations Territory, whose future seemed predestined when she received her name, Karon Hiawi. It means "She Carries the Sky." To see her dance, one might be forgiven for believing that she is, indeed, carrying the sky. A dancer of formidable talent, Santee received her training at the National Ballet School. A desire to explore other forms of dance and perhaps to explore a marriage of dance vocabularies — that of ballet with the traditional form of Plains dancing now seen at pow-wows — led Santee to other choreographers and dance projects.

Santee performed with the Aboriginal Dance Project at the Banff Centre for the Arts in a program entitled *Chinook Winds*. She has since choreographed and performed her own work, most notably at the Canadian Aboriginal Festival in Toronto in 1997. To add to her performance art repertoire, Santee has taken theatre training to prepare herself for dramatic roles, in addition to those that focus on dance.

A skilled potter, Santee learned the craft under the watchful eyes of her parents, renowned Mohawk potters Leigh and Steven Smith. She now produces traditional and contemporary Iroquois pottery that is shown in galleries such as the Woodland Cultural Museum in Brantford and the National Museum of Civilization in Hull, Quebec. The work Santee creates is prized and praised and has earned her awards in art competitions in Oklahoma and in Connecticut.

Santee is a new mother now, having welcomed a baby girl into the family in 1998. Perhaps another in a long line of gifted artists, each of whom, in their turn, passed on the skill and the passion for a timeless art.

Will she dance again? It will be a welcome sight to see. We must wait patiently for the day when we can gather and watch Santee Smith as — with poise and ineffable grace — she carries the sky.

ANDREW MARACLE ～

Andrew Maracle was one of eight children born on the Six Nations Territory to Margaret Lickers and Joseph W. Maracle. After the death of his wife, Joseph returned to the Tyendinaga Reserve with his youngest son.

As a young man with growing faith in the divine word, Andrew entered divinity school to study for ordination. While pursuing his studies, he visited the Zion Bible Institute in Providence, Rhode Island, as a student speaker, and there he met the woman who later became his wife. They were married for sixty years and had six sons.

After receiving his Doctor of Divinity degree, Andrew returned to Tyendinaga with his wife, Lillian, to preach his ministry. He founded the Assembly of God there, as well as a small business selling Native crafts. Andrew was a self-made man who often said: "I can only achieve according to the effort that I infuse into what I believe." He was a man of many beliefs, but one faith.

On February 8, 1999, in his eighty-ninth year, Reverend Andrew C. Maracle, Sr., passed on. Tyendinaga mourned the loss of its most distinguished Mohawk Speaker.

A Mohawk of the Turtle Clan, Andrew was named Ka ron hiak tatie, which means "Along the Heavens."

DOROTHY GREEN ~

At eighty, Dorothy Green is the oldest member of the Onondaga Longhouse. A child of Cayuga parents, she explains, "I went to the Onondaga Longhouse as a kid, because my dad used to take us. That's the one I got used to." She served as a faithkeeper for many years, attending all the ceremonies, singing the songs and dancing the dances, until arthritis stilled her movements.

After some schooling at the Mohawk Institute Residential School, she went to live with her grandparents and work on the family farm. A young man came to work there, and in no time, he had proposed to Dorothy. They married and had a family of nine, providing for them from their labors on the farm. Now widowed, Dorothy is grandmother to thirty, great-grandmother to fifty, and great-great-grandmother to one.

Dorothy has a dandy skill. Working with deer and moose hides, she makes moccasins, jackets, and leggings, and at eighty, the "moccasin lady" is still busy filling orders.

Dorothy, a Cayuga of the Turtle Clan, is named Kiduwitu. It means "Walking in Gardens," which is what she did, all her life.

HUBERT SKY ~

When Hubert Sky was a student, he fell under the influence of a powerful role model: J.C. Hill, a teacher and home-town hero. Hubert followed in his footsteps. He got a teaching certificate and spent the next thirty-four years teaching elementary school.

While teaching in Moose Factory, he met a young Cree woman from Saskatchewan who had come to the school as a cook. They courted and married, and Hubert brought Bertha Sky home to the Six Nations Territory, where they have enjoyed forty-two years of bliss and the company of five children.

In the years that nurtured and shaped Hubert, he had the good fortune to have, as parents, two Longhouse followers. His mother, a Cayuga who was fluent in her language, was a clan mother; his father, a faithkeeper, was fluent in his language, Onondaga. Hubert learned their languages and went on to gain an understanding of the remaining four Iroquoian languages: Seneca, Mohawk, Tuscarora, and Oneida.

Oratory is the centerpiece of the Longhouse ceremony, because it is the speeches, carefully rendered, that give expression to the religious ideas of the Longhouse. Nothing is written down; the speeches can be learned only by listening to them, by hearing them over and over again. For the last two years, Hubert has been teaching the young men the speeches "that we learn in the Longhouse, because we are running out of speakers. It's really needed to keep the traditional religion going."

There are seventeen Longhouse ceremonies throughout the year that need speakers like Hubert, and as interest in the traditional teachings continues, an increasing number of couples are choosing to marry in the Longhouse. By his tally, Hubert has married nearly three hundred couples in the last twenty years.

Hubert Sky, a Cayuga of the Snipe Clan, is named Sugowunta, which means "Goal Scorer."

A prayer of thanksgiving, an *Adó:wa*, was sung for him at the Naming Ceremony, and the Speaker asked for the blessings of a long and useful life. And the Creator listened.

In circles we gather / Moonlight fires are kindled
Sending it back / We just make it go back
Beating hearts, beating hearts

— ROBBIE ROBERTSON

CODY MOORE ～

Certainty is a trademark of youth. We say that. We remember how sure we were of everything when we were young. It was a warm, secure feeling that stemmed from our inability to look at things from all sides. Sure. And then along comes a kid like Cody Moore. Fifteen years old. A Grade Eleven student who enrolled himself in a parochial high school because it offered a better program. Like any wise consumer, he did comparison shopping for his education and made a value judgment.

Cody Moore has plans. He is a promising art student with a keen interest in computer graphics. To finance his education, he is prepared to do two years of military service. This is a thoughtful, pragmatic, some would say grown-up, approach. But here's the kid part: Cody wants to design video games. To finance the extras that are so essential to a boy's enjoyment of life, the electronic games and his kick-boxing stuff, Cody spent the summer as a hired hand in Essex County. He planted corn.

Pow-wow dancing is a family affair. Like his father, Cody dances in the traditional style. Now a seasoned performer with more than a dozen years of dancing behind him, his movements are sure and effortless and full of the nuance that comes with a clear understanding of understatement, that elusive place in traditional dance where its art resides.

An independent boy who enjoys solitude, Cody spends a lot of his time in his own company. Like other boys, he uses the time to play Nintendo games. Knowing a little about him, it is easy to imagine that he is also thinking and planning and arriving at certainties.

A Pima/Oneida of the Bear Clan, Cody was given the middle name Little Shadow.

FRED WILLIAMS ~ Fred Williams has been working virtually all his life. The only

child of parents who traveled the continent performing in Wild West shows, he took his first bow at the tender age of a year and a half. Fred's parents toured with Wild Bill Cody and played out the opening of the American West in villages and burgs throughout Europe.

As Fred grew, he took on a more active role, literally. He rode steers. "Then I got bigger and so did the steers," he said, recalling the early rodeo days. "The trick was to try and stay on." These tests of a man's mettle ended when Fred was called up to face a more daunting challenge: World War II. Drafted by the U.S. military, he served in the South Pacific.

By war's end, Wild West shows had seen their heyday. A Mohawk of the Wolf Clan, Fred came home to the Six Nations Territory in 1955, took up welding, and spent the next thirty-two years making farm equipment. He married a faithkeeper in the Longhouse, and together they had seven children.

From those early rodeo days, Fred took away a treasure of a trick. He mastered the bullwhip. Picture, if you will, Fred's bullwhip slicing paper held between the lips of a trusting soul. No magic. No mirrors. Just artistry.

Fred has the name Go Wah Ha Ga Ho, which means "Flowers Lying on the Ground."

Going home, going home
To a nation, six nations
To all the faces I did not know
Beating hearts, beating hearts

— ROBBIE ROBERTSON

ESTHER SUNDOWN ~ The daughter of a Seneca chief, born on the Tonawanda

Reservation in New York State, Esther Sundown grew up in a world filled with chiefs, clan mothers, and faithkeepers. She learned the traditions of the Longhouse at a very tender age, and to this day, she enjoys a life enriched by cultural observances.

Her parents resisted sending Esther to school to learn English, and though they ultimately relented, they did so with a fair dose of skepticism. She stayed to the Fifth Grade. At age nine, she had her first exposure to midwifery, assisting her grandmother. She subsequently learned enough about the practice to deliver babies on her own and continued her work well into her seventies.

When she arrived at a marriageable age, she was paired off with a man she didn't know, so she refused for a long time to consummate the marriage, taking shelter under various roofs other than the one he offered. She doesn't say what changed her mind. In the course of her married life, she had five children.

When speaking of her age, Esther said, "I give the Creator a big thanks for that. He is taking care of me."

BRIAN GENERAL ∿

Brian General dances every day, for a living. Terenge Huata, a New Zealander who was interested in forming a theatrical dance troupe, saw Brian dancing at a pow-wow on the Six Nations Territory and hired him right out of high school. That was five years ago. As a fledgling company, the Kanata Native Dance Theatre traveled across Canada, visiting First Nations communities in the Prairies and on the west coast, and learning their dances. In return, the troupe performed the Iroquois social dances. It was a cultural exchange that expanded the troupe's repertoire of traditional dance.

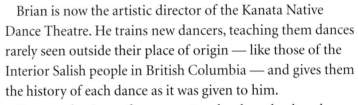

Brian is now the artistic director of the Kanata Native Dance Theatre. He trains new dancers, teaching them dances rarely seen outside their place of origin — like those of the Interior Salish people in British Columbia — and gives them the history of each dance as it was given to him.

Kanata takes its performances to schools and cultural gatherings all over North America. This spring, Brian toured schools in California where his troupe took its traditional Native dances to audiences that were mostly Hispanic. For Brian, these performances are a way to shatter the stereotypical image of the Indian as savage, to show that he is a spiritual man with respect for others and for what he has been given.

A Seneca of the Turtle Clan, Brian is the son of a Longhouse chief and a faithkeeper, guardians of the Iroquois traditions, and he is quick to acknowledge that they have had the biggest influence on his life. Two years ago, he was asked to be a worker — to assist the faithkeepers — at the feast following the Medicine Mask Rites that are held every spring. To Brian, this was a great honor.

Brian is named Sowa:has, which means "Tall Flower."

FLINT EAGLE ~

Flint Eagle has appeared in seventy-one films, as an actor and stunt performer. He designs clothes and has five lines currently on the market. These accomplishments are quickly set aside, however, as he talks about building a foreign Aboriginal cultural embassy at his reserve at Kahnewake. The idea took form while he was in Taiwan, meeting the Indigenous people in that country.

He describes his mandate: "To unite Aboriginal people of the world in an effort to bring an exchange of culture, traditions, education, economic, and social development in friendship and peace, in accordance with the *Kaswentha* — the Two-Row Wampum."

Flint is a child of parents whose brief lives were, in fact, larger than life. They were both professional wrestlers. He was orphaned at the age of five and sent to live in Florida with his maternal grandmother. After college, he was called home because his paternal grandmother was ailing. Flint counts as a blessing the time they spent together before she passed on.

"I am learning to be true to what the Creator intended me to be," says Flint. "The Creator intended me to be a Mohawk; therefore, I must be the best Mohawk I can be. Otherwise, I am in danger of being nothing."

Flint is named Tioronhiate, which means "Bright Blue Sky."

HUBERT BUCK ~ There are many songs in the Longhouse litany: songs of rejoicing,

songs of hope that goodness will continue, and songs of thanksgiving to the Creator and to all the helpers who have provided a bountiful harvest. There are personal songs, created by the individual to express reverence and thanks. Hubert Buck's gift is song. As a member of the singing collective Ojihgwagayohn he sings in the Longhouse and at socials.

Hubert is the only surviving son of a family of four daughters and two sons. He was born to parents who gave him a childhood rich in tradition — infused with the ritual observances of the Longhouse and the sounds and cadence of the Seneca language.

These days, Hubert sets forth from the family home with its lingering echoes of a time long past, and he drives to Kaweni:io, a high school on the Six Nations Territory, and directs his steps to the computer room. There, waiting for him, is a throng of students eager to make acquaintance with the technology that will carry them into the new century. Hubert will teach them. It is his gift to them.

Hubert is a member of the Turtle Clan. He is named Twesgyco, a Seneca word that describes the action of a walking person who is stepping into a run.

RYAN BURNHAM ～ The tyke in the Plains-style headdress is eight years old now.
He's a Third Grade student at Emily C. General public school on the Six Nations Territory who has already distinguished himself as something of a math whiz by scoring the highest mark in Grade Two testing.

Ryan Burnham also has an appetite for sports. In winter, when the ice freezes and the snows are deep, he plays hockey and skis cross-country. Spring months are given over to track and field competition, and in the summer, he visits the greens for rounds of golf with his dad. At the age of three, he started lacrosse in the paperweight division of the Six Nations minor lacrosse system. Every summer he takes to the field with his lacrosse stick in hand and plays the ancestral game under the watchful eyes of his grandparents, who rarely miss a match.

Ryan is a boy with designs on dentistry, who marks every trip to the dentist as an opportunity to pepper the doctor with professional questions in the manner of one who is giving serious consideration to the practice as a future occupation. He is often heard promising his future to dentistry. Then, especially after a day filled with the fun of teeing off and putting, he abandons dentistry for dreams of golfing fame.

This much holds true. Ryan is a boy who has unwavering designs on life.

CHRISTINA BOMBERRY ⁓ Fortune has certainly smiled on Christina

Bomberry. It has smiled often and in many ways. It has opened its arms and carried her aloft to distant places — to Europe and Asia. She has promoted the fashions of Simon Chang and the culture of the Iroquois, in Taiwan. As a member of the Kanata Dance Theatre, she has presented Aboriginal dances in concert, in Italy.

Christina attended grade school on the Six Nations Territory and high school in Caledonia, a short

bus ride from her home. She had a typical childhood that included an abundance of time with her grandmother. Though not a dancer herself, Grandma, enamored of the western style of pow-wow dancing, encouraged Christina to try, and showed her, as best she could, how the steps were done. But to dance, one also needs an outfit. In that area, Grandma was on firm ground. She taught Christina and together they set about the task of sewing a dress and fancy shawl. There must have been magic in those hours; Christina grew to love sewing as much as dancing.

Christina's grandmother had more to give beyond tips in dancing and sewing. She was full of good advice and very generous with it. It may be that the first strains of language in the Cayuga tongue that Christina heard came from her grandmother.

Christina has a baby girl named Jadyn who will soon celebrate her first birthday. Jadyn has been to the Longhouse to receive her name. In the years ahead and in accordance with custom, Christina will pass on to Jadyn all the teachings she received from her own parents and grandparents. And the first strains of the Cayuga tongue that Jadyn will hear will come from Christina.

Fortune has smiled again.

Christina's mother is Mohawk and her father is Onondaga. She is named Cohwenah. It is a name that resides with the Turtle Clan, and it means "Paddling Down River on Canoe."

AMOS KEY, JR. 〜 Amos Key, Jr., is in love with language, and it comes as no surprise.

His grandmother knew this, and that is why Susan Jamieson gave Amos the name He Splits Words. The son of a Mohawk mother who knew three tongues and a Cayuga father who was fluent in four, Amos remembers the lingual gymnastics of parents who switched languages in the way that many Europeans do.

With each new winter come the Midwinter Ceremonies, eight days of giving thanks and rejoicing in Creation. Amos, in his role as faithkeeper, honors the timeless tradition of oration, of calling the people to the Sunrise Ceremonies, of calling the people to put away work, games, and amusements and to give over their thoughts to the Renewal Ceremony.

He has recorded verbatim all the Seneca Longhouse speeches, and he currently chairs the Cayuga Dictionary and Grammar Development Project. For the last fifteen years, he has directed the First Nations Languages Program at the Woodland Cultural Centre in Brantford, Ontario. He also developed a community radio station CKRZ, at Six Nations Territory, which proved to be a ground-breaking achievement and one that other First Nations communities would later follow.

The last words should go to He Splits Words. "When I look at my people, I look at the whole landscape. What will we protect and keep? What are the institutions and the customs we will keep? Those are the questions of the day. What infrastructure do we need to preserve a traditional life in the dominant society? I think of the Two-Row Wampum and the challenge to be in one canoe or the other. And then I think of the catamaran with its two hulls." It is a suitable metaphor for a man who straddles both worlds and never loses his balance.

HANNA GENERAL ~ Hanna General lived off the land and she lived for the land,
planting, nurturing, and harvesting its offerings. For Hanna, each year could be divided neatly into two
parts: the season when the earth did its work and the season when it rested. She was a farm child.

When she grew older, she never missed an opportunity to do a little more work for a few dollars,
which is how she met her husband. He was a bachelor with laundry.

In the months when the earth rested, Hanna made things. She made everything from quilts to lemon
pies. One of her quilts was chosen as a bicentennial gift to the U.S. president, and some of her beadwork
is in a time capsule in Toronto.

Hanna General knew sorrow. She buried a son. Better than most, she understood that everything has
a season. Raised by traditional Longhouse parents, Hanna, a Cayuga of the Wolf Clan, stayed close to
the Longhouse all her life. She received the name Kahdeyus, which means "Cut the Forest."

In the graveyards of the Longhouse, there are no headstones to weigh down the spirit. At Hanna's
place, there is a magnolia tree.

DYLAN ISAACS ～

Dylan Isaacs was born into a family that is fully immersed in Iroquois culture. He sings the songs he hears his mother sing, so his repertoire of Iroquois songs is growing. His mother is one of the Six Nations Women Singers, a group that performs professionally. Dylan dances too. His grandfather, Jim Sky, leads a group that performs traditional Iroquois dance, so Dylan learned to dance at a tender age. Now he is learning the language. He attends a primary school on the Six Nations Territory, where Cayuga is taught.

Dylan's grandmother, Lizzie Silversmith, chose his name, and he received it during the Harvest Festival. An *Adó:wa* was sung for him, as is done for all male children as part of their Naming Ceremony.

To mark the occasion, he received a pair of hide moccasins, beaded for him by his father.

Dylan's Cayuga name is Tohnyawes, a name that resides with the Bear Clan. It means "Splitting the Sky."

I can't let go of the old way / I can't let go of the ancient ways
It's in the blood I can't let go / It's in the blood
It's in the blood I can't let go

— Robbie Robertson

ALVIN PARKER 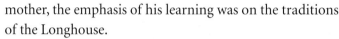 It is hard to distinguish this modern-day Seneca from the spirits of his ancestors, who hold such a presence within him. His stories move freely from the exploits of his parents to those of revered uncles, whose deeds in times long past could only have been described to him.

Al's parents were Senecas; his mother came from Tonawanda, which had a Longhouse tradition, and his father came from Cattaraugus, which had an electoral system. Al understood both systems of governance, but as his mother's ties to the Longhouse were strengthened by her role in it as a clan

mother, the emphasis of his learning was on the traditions of the Longhouse.

Self-described as a late bloomer, Al married and had a family before enrolling in Buffalo State College for a degree in Education. He was in his thirties and thoroughly motivated to be educated and to educate. In addition to fulfilling the role he describes as "the bread and butter guy," Al volunteers to teach Native culture. He has also helped to promote and market a CD on the Great Law of Peace that was produced at Six Nations.

He dances at pow-wows and is easily distinguished by his traditional Longhouse outfit. It elicits interest and often results in invitations to speak about the Iroquoian culture and traditions.

An ancestor that Al brings vividly to life is Elie S. Parker, a condoled sachem, with a background in engineering, who later became a brigadier-general in the U.S. Army and a friend of Yankee general Ulysses S. Grant. Grant called upon Parker, who possessed a fine hand at penmanship, to write out the surrender terms that ended the American Civil War. The American Indian Science and Engineering Society gives an annual award in the name of Elie S. Parker. As his descendant, Al has been proud to make the presentation.

Al's name, Ho yen dah onh, once belonged to an uncle, a skilled woodcarver, whose work is in the Rochester Museum of Science. It is a name from the Heron Clan and it means "He Got It."

PERRY POINT ~ Perry Point is a student at General Vanier Secondary School in
Cornwall, where he excels in Native studies. He speaks Mohawk and credits his grandparents, who
taught him the language as a child. He values it as a great gift from them. It is a gift that serves him well
as a Longhouse participant. He is learning to sing the ceremonial songs, which are complex choral
structures with many verses.

One summer, he worked with the North American Indian Travelling College in recreating an ancient
Longhouse. But much of Perry's summers are now given over to the pow-wow gatherings that take place
on reserves every weekend. He competes as a grass dancer in an outfit made with the help of an aunt
and a cousin. An older sister beaded a headdress for him.

When asked about his hopes for the future, he replied, "I hope that the language will survive." By
speaking Mohawk himself, he is helping to ensure the future and vitality of the language. In the years
ahead, the community will look to him to pass on his gift from his grandparents to his children.

Perry is a Mohawk of the Wolf Clan who is named Kakwirakeron. It means "Standing Pine."

MELISSA PARKER ∼ Melissa Parker wants to be a pharmacist — not such a surprising choice for a girl whose brother grows Indian medicines.

A student at Mount Mercy High School in Buffalo and a budding actress, Melissa appeared in the Mount Mercy production of *Do Black Patent Leather Shoes Really Reflect Up?* Her father, Al Parker, caught it all on tape.

The art of performance plays a major role in Melissa's life. She dances with the Buffalo Creek Dance Group, who specialize in the Iroquois social dances. She is a prize-winning jingle-dress dancer at competition pow-wows who began dancing at the age of four.

She attends the Tonawanda Longhouse and understands the ceremonies that are conducted in the Seneca language.

Melissa Parker is fourteen years old. She got her first haircut a few months ago. Nothing drastic. Only a few inches. Just enough to traumatize her Dad.

CLEVELAND GENERAL ∼ Cleveland General is a living repository for the

centuries-old ritual formalities of the Longhouse ceremonies that are passed from memory to memory.

This was not always the case. Cleveland was named hereditary chief at the age of twenty-eight. Not ready for the role thrust upon him, he left the Six Nations Territory and the Longhouse in pursuit of work in high steel. The hunt took him to cities in Canada and the United States and onto the breezy

skeletal structures of buildings in their primitive states. He finished his working life on the pipeline "because it was on the ground."

In Cleveland's mother, the Cayuga language found constant expression. She guaranteed its fluency and prepared Cleveland for the role that awaited him. The elders prepared him, as well. "When the elders were still living, I learned a lot by just listening," says Cleveland. "I knew that I would have to do it one day."

Now, he teaches the children and he teaches the parents. He is consulted by growing numbers of young people eager to learn, to listen, and to take into their memory the words of the Longhouse. They need the language to achieve this, so Cleveland is teaching them his mother's tongue.

In the Longhouse calendar, there are many ceremonies. Some are reassuringly predictable, coinciding with plantings and harvests. Others occur by chance: the marriages and burials that mark the beginnings and endings of lives. Cleveland speaks of the burials: "At the grave, when someone passes on, I take their name off and sit it on the ground. One year after that, the family can use that name again. Ten days from the burial, they have a feast for the one that is gone and all the useful things must be given out to his family and friends."

At seventy-five, Cleveland is in the full embrace of a destiny envisioned by the ancestors who named him hereditary chief nearly fifty years ago. He listened. He caught the words and shaped them into an understanding. And he has held it all in his memory for those who will listen.

85

TSIONATIIO ～

(CENTRE) Tsionatiio speaks Mohawk all day. Even in the playground, all the gleeful shouts are in Mohawk. Complete immersion in the language and its construction is paramount at Akwesasne Freedom School, a private school situated on the U.S. side of the Akwesasne Reserve.

When school is out, Tsionatiio takes lessons in jazz dancing and tap. She is also a member of the Akwesasne Figure Skating Club and took part in its third annual ice show, an extravaganza memorably named *Akwesasne Goes Hollywood*.

Before Tsionatiio's arrival, her parents consulted with the clan mothers of the Bear Clan to discover what names were available. They chose Tsionatiio — and they chose only Tsionatiio. She has no English name. At the first Harvest Festival after her birth, she visited the Longhouse to receive her name. Since then, she has attended many more Naming Ceremonies and has watched as other newcomers made their first visits to the Longhouse.

In describing her, one might be compelled to say, "She Beautifies the Village." In the Mohawk language, the name for that expression is Tsionatiio.

OKIOKWINON ～

(LEFT) Okiokwinon has the English name Chelsea Francis. Now eight years old, Okiokwinon is in Grade Three at the Akwesasne Freedom School. When school is over for the day, she likes to ride her bicycle and swim.

She also likes to go to the ceremonies at the Longhouse.

KAHENTAHAWIH ～

(RIGHT) Kahentahawih, whose English name is Chelsea Francis, is six years old and in the First Grade at the Akwesasne Freedom School, where the only language spoken in the classrooms and on the playground is Mohawk. Kahentahawih is learning to read and to write in her native tongue.

She dances at socials and likes to take walks in the evenings with her Dad.

WATENWANAHAWI:THA ~ Watenwanahawi:tha, whose English name

is Chantelle Francis, is a young woman of tender years — she has just entered her teenhood — and well-formed ideas. She wants to be a pediatrician and work on her own reserve, Akwesasne. She wants "to get the language back and for more of the people to have knowledge of the medicines and of how to conduct the ceremonies, so that our culture doesn't die."

Watenwanahawi:tha is often asked to help at special ceremonies at the Longhouse and has been to many traditional weddings, which she was eager to describe: "The bride and groom have baskets. The bride has cornbread and cloth in her basket, to show that she will cook and clean for him, and the groom has venison and leather and sweetgrass, to show that he will provide her with food and clothing. And they exchange baskets."

It was just two years ago that Watenwanahawi:tha received her name from the clan mothers. It means "Within She Carries Her Voice." Next autumn, she will attend high school off reserve in Massena, New York, and to students unaccustomed to the multisyllabic Mohawk names, she will be Chantelle Francis. To Chantelle, she will be Watenwanahawi:tha, a Mohawk of the Turtle Clan.

STEVE MONTOUR ~ For more than a decade, Steve Montour has been working
in his own backyard. He has been a peacekeeper with the Six Nations Territory police force since 1985,
when it was in its infancy. Today the peacekeepers make up one of the leading forces in Ontario, but
Steve would like to see the day when the force will no longer be needed. As he puts it, "My personal goal
is that everybody would return to the traditional way of thinking and I would be out of a job, which
would be a good thing."

It was the traditional way of thinking that shaped the lives of Lillian and Cecil Montour and guided
them in their roles as parents to Steve, his four brothers, and his sister. His grandparents were ever
present, full of stories and possessed of a boundless capacity for listening to what the children had
to say, which, in itself, spoke volumes to them.

When he thinks of the future and what it will offer his daughters, he speaks of a need for entrepre-
neurship and economic growth at Six Nations. A betting sort might wager that Steve will, in time to
come, arm himself with an economics degree, develop a new idea, and hang out a shingle that says:
"Open for business."

Steve, a Mohawk of the Turtle Clan, is named Al>sohonyons. It means "Splitting the Sky."

Going away to where I'm from
Find my way back within the circle
Listen to the learned, the tattooed and the scarred
Listen to the questions, not the answers

— ROBBIE ROBERTSON

ARNOLD GENERAL ~

Arnold General is an Onondaga who speaks Cayuga and has an understanding of the Mohawk, Onondaga, and Tuscarora languages. His traditional teachings began early and came from an adoptive father who was a faithkeeper in the Sour Springs Longhouse at Six Nations. As a young boy, with a mother ill and hospitalized in a sanatorium, Arnold was left in the care of his adoptive father and uncle, who spoke only Cayuga. As he puts it, he was "involved in the language from day one."

He advises on languages and cultural teaching at McMaster University in Hamilton, Ontario, and he participates in an advocacy program for elders at McMaster Medical Centre. When death occurs, Arnold is called upon to release the spirit.

A chief and speaker in the Longhouse, Arnold serves his community as he believes he was meant to do. Once troubled by the prophecy of a chief who feared "we would lose our ways in time," Arnold has had a lighter heart of late, seeing so many young people eager to learn the teachings; the average age at the Longhouse ceremonies, for which there is sometimes standing room only, is twenty-two.

Of the Great Law, Arnold has this to say: "It is based on common sense and on respecting what the Creator gave us." And he views the sustainability of wildlife in wildlife corridors as an urgent concern. Intimate communion with all living things is a hallmark of a traditional life.

Of all the teachings Arnold General has received, perhaps it is the words of his grandmother that have the greatest resonance. "Everybody comes through good and bad. With determination, you can do whatever you need to do, if you have to." There are many things Arnold General just has to do.

Arnold, an Onondaga of the Beaver Clan, is named Dahutgadons. It means "Looking Both Ways."

RICHARD MITCHELL ~

Richard Mitchell has been preparing all of his life for his role as wampum keeper for the Mohawk Nation Longhouse at Akwesasne. His boyhood was spent learning the values that form the foundation of Longhouse thought. His life has been spent in the practice of what he learned as a child. In acknowledgment of this, he was asked by his community to be their wampum keeper. Feeling that he was not sufficiently learned at the time, he agreed to do it, but only temporarily. He applied himself diligently to fulfilling the role, and after three years, he was selected to be the wampum keeper for all the five nations: Mohawk, Seneca, Cayuga, Oneida, and Onondaga.

To understand that the history of the Great Law of Peace is preserved in the wampum gives one a fuller appreciation of the honor conferred on Richard. It is the wampum keeper who carries the nation's history to all the ceremonies.

At first glance, Richard's life experiences mirror those of countless Mohawk men. In the days of his youth, he was a star lacrosse player. Of his breadwinning years, twenty-five were spent as an iron worker. Interwoven with these endeavors is a lifelong study of the founding principles and laws of governance contained within the Iroquois Great Law of Peace and of the rites and rituals of the Longhouse. He is a man committed to his family — he and his wife of thirty-four years have five sons — and to his community.

There are few speakers who can recite the Code of Handsome Lake. Richard is one of them. In the Longhouse calendar, time is set aside in late October for the Recitation of the Code. The week-long ceremony is conducted at each of five of the Longhouses within the Confederacy. The five remaining Longhouses will host the ceremonies the following year. As wampum keeper, Richard will carry the wampum to all five Longhouses at which the Code of Handsome Lake will be heard, and it may well be Richard that the people hear.

A member of the Wolf Clan, Richard is named Aroniatekha, which means "Burning Sky."

MARK PORTER ～

Mark Porter is an instrument of cultural exchange, a finely tuned instrument with a memory of countless dances that strike the right notes with audiences all over the continent. The Kanata Native Dance Theatre has in its repertoire playful dances full of visual wit, in which dancers reinvent themselves as birds, butterflies, and horses full of frenzy. Mark is one of those gifted dancers.

He has traveled everywhere, learning new dances and leaving old ones that fresh eyes make new. And he has taken dance to the steamy asphalt and concrete of inner-city America, where little is concrete, save need. He has presented the splendor of Native dance to children in the schools there. Mark took the heartbeat to children raised on the pulsating rhythms of salsa. They had plenty of questions to ask.

Mark is always prepared. He is well trained. He knows his subject, and before executing a single movement in performance, Mark learned to think on his feet. He is shaping a life of joyful purpose, helping in the migration of stories told in dance.

Mark, an Oneida of the Turtle Clan, is named Mishgogabwe wawashka nini, which means "Standing Strong Dear Man."

TIA SMITH ～

No one is more aptly suited to the role of teaching than Tia Smith. Because teaching involves talking, a lot of talking, and because talking is something she does well, she'll be perfect. That it's her strong suit is evident from the first hello. Her push-button memory, especially for detail, lets her give vivid descriptions of experiences that many might consider too banal for storage. In conversation, her facility with language can send stories tumbling from her memory in an engaging free fall. Tia simply gets more out of life.

After playing field lacrosse for the home team for one year, Tia tried out for the provincial team. This speaks volumes about her skill at the game. She brushes it off: "It kinda comes naturally to the Native girls around here."

To Tia's grandparents, her birth signaled the arrival of their much-awaited first grandchild, and an exceptional bond exists between them. "Never settle," her grandfather told her. "Always be the best you can be." Ever mindful, she is doing just that.

Tia, a Cayuga of the Wolf Clan, is named Saneyahwas, which means "Looking for the Name."

JIM SKY ～

No word describes Jim Sky better than *teacher*. He is perhaps best known as the leader of the Jim Sky Dancers, a group loosely composed of family members who present the social dances of the Iroquois. Each dance is preceded by Jim's description of the dance and its history. He's been teaching in this way for almost thirty years.

He himself had good teachers. Jim's parents were Longhouse people, rooted in tradition, each possessed of a good mind and a Native tongue, who taught their children well. Times being what they were, Jim didn't get to high school. In fact, he didn't go past the fifth grade. But Jim didn't need school to learn to understand all the Iroquoian languages, as he does. He is a fluent speaker of two: Onondaga and Cayuga.

For the most part, Jim Sky did not lead the genteel life of an educator. He was a working man in toil that exacted a physical toll, a family man with children to feed, who acquired skills in welding and auto mechanics to trade on as a breadwinner. He worked hard and prospered. He bought quarter-horses and taught his children the intricacies of riding, executing figure eights and other tricky maneuvers. Neighborhood children flocked to the Sky house, wanting to ride, and they learned too. It is easy to imagine Jim's home resonating with the laughter and squeals of children when their excitement reached full throttle. After his children had grown and the laughter died down, he waited patiently for grandchildren to usher in a new cycle of sounds.

Soon it will be time for another ceremony. As he has done for many years, Jim Sky, a faithkeeper for the Onondaga Longhouse, will see that there is wood cut for the fire and that all is made ready to receive the people. Then, Jim Sky, as one of the few speakers in the Onondaga Longhouse, will address the people.

An Onondaga of the Deer Clan, Jim is named Hiwhageh, which means "Finding a Way."

DANIEL DAVID MOSES ～ Daniel David Moses is a poet and playwright
whose work reveals a luminous intelligence and lyricism. Writing from a Native perspective, he has produced a body of work — two volumes of poetry and ten plays — that has earned him acclaim from within the Native communities across the country and beyond, from a mainstream theatre-going public.

Delicate Bodies, Daniel's first collection of poetry, was published in 1980. Following this, he turned his attention to playwriting and wrote *Coyote City*, which earned him a nomination for the Governor General's Award. More plays followed, and with each one, he broke new ground and garnered more prizes.

Daniel began his life on the Six Nations Territory. The son of a Tuscarora mother and Delaware father, he remained at home throughout his junior and senior school years. After graduation, he left to pursue a degree in Fine Arts at York University in Toronto. Later, he moved on to the University of British Columbia, where he was accorded a Master's degree in writing. Though he now lives in Toronto, Daniel's roots are firmly bedded in home soil.

Daniel David Moses is a native son who speaks a language that is universally understood.

ROBERTA JAMIESON ~ Roberta Jamieson's position in the vanguard of

Aboriginal representation in the area of law and justice is inarguable. The first woman from a First Nation in Ontario to earn a law degree, the first non-parliamentarian to serve as an ex-officio member of the Special House of Commons Committee on Indian Self-Government, and the first woman to be appointed as Ombudsman in Ontario: these facts when taken together are sufficient to make the case.

Her lectures and papers on alternative methods of dispute resolution have earned recognition and awards. She has received the Order of Canada, a National Aboriginal Achievement Award, and six honorary Doctorates of Law from universities across Canada.

Roberta was educated at a primary school on the Six Nations Territory at a time when English held supremacy in the classroom. That is no longer true. Through the efforts of Roberta, working in consort with like-minded people at Six Nations, the Iroquoian languages are an integral part of education in the community.

When one takes into account the milestones in Roberta's career in jurisprudence, it comes as a surprise to know that she did it all without leaving home. A Mohawk daughter with roots firmly planted, she is of the Bear Clan and lives at Six Nations with her husband, Tom Hill.

MIKE MITCHELL ∼

When Mike's parents moved to Cornwall Island, he stayed behind with his grandparents, at St. Regis. They were traditional Mohawks who taught him the language, the songs, and the ceremonies of the Longhouse. He was late starting school and when he did start attending, he spoke no English at all. When a priest asked Mike who he was, he replied, "I am Kanen takeron and I am Longhouse." "I got the shock of my life," says Mike, "when he grabbed me by the ear and told the kids I was a pagan. I stole a boat and went back to the island." He did return to the school, and he excelled there, but still remained unapologetically Longhouse.

He joined the National Film Board of Canada in his early twenties and seemed destined for a career as a filmmaker. His old friend and mentor, Ernie Benedict, who had earlier started the North American Indian Travelling College as a cultural college on wheels, urged him to restart the defunct college with its fleet of three vans. (They contained books for distribution, but were suffering from flat tires.) Within a year, the college was up and running again — and Mike had added an audio-visual department.

As elected grand chief of the Akwesasne Mohawk Council, Mike Mitchell has taken a community on the brink of receivership to one with an operating budget that is close to sixty million dollars and with programs designed and implemented by the people. He has been re-elected five times. His leadership gets a resolute round of applause.

Mike Mitchell has waged a long struggle in the courts for recognition of the Aboriginal right to trade freely across the border. After ten years of legal wrangling, he got his day in court and won. However, the victory was fleeting, as the case is under appeal.

Mike, pictured here with the young Mohawk athlete Corey Thomas, received the name Kanentakeron. It is a name of the Wolf Clan, and it means "Many Pine Trees Falling."

DONALD WHITE, JR. ~ Donald White, Jr., descends from a long line of

Mohawk traditionalists. His maternal grandmother, famed basket maker Eva Point, was a clan mother and his grandfather Louis was a faithkeeper. They gave him many gifts. It was his grandfather who gave him the Smoke Dance, an Iroquois social dance that has become Donald's specialty and one that he teaches to children. Donald's love of dance includes pow-wow dancing, and he travels to gatherings all over Ontario, Quebec, and New York State to compete as a traditional dancer. His dancing won him a part in the movie *Grey Owl*.

The only son of Longhouse parents, he was given the name of his mother's twin brother, who had passed away. In a Naming Ceremony, he received the name Kanerahtiio, which means "Medicine Leaf." It resides with the Wolf Clan.

Donald takes pride in his parents' achievements. He describes his mother's work as an artist, illustrating curriculum texts for use in Mohawk language studies — and he talks about the beef cattle on the family farm, which his father operates.

Donald was a member of a boxing club and fought in tournaments. When it conflicted with his pow-wow dancing, he made a decision. He put the circle before the ring.

Oh, listen for the night chant
Oh, listen for the night chant

— ROBBIE ROBERTSON

BERNICE LAZORE ～ For Bernice Lazore, retirement lasted five months.

When the Mohawk Council of Akwesasne advertised a six-month contract position in its Archival Department, she applied for the job. That was three years ago. Bernice is now on loan to Aboriginal Lands, Rights and Research, working in consultation with elders in a job in which Mohawk is a must.

Although her parents left the church in favor of the Longhouse when she was twelve, she remains an active church member and is involved in a movement to confer sainthood on Kateri Dekakwitha, an Algonquin who was beatified in Rome in 1980. Bernice attends the Longhouse, too, for the ceremonies that are held throughout the year.

One can see the dichotomy, but Bernice has found an accommodation within that provides room for both — blending traditional spirituality with Christian beliefs.

When Bernice was an infant, her father gave her the name of his mother; however, her grandmother was a member of the Snipe Clan, and Bernice, following her mother, was of the Wolf Clan. "I went to the Naming Ceremony, and the clan mothers gave me a new Wolf name. My cousin, who was Snipe, took the name my father had picked." The clan mothers chose Kasennororon for Bernice. It means "Precious Name."

And when you see the sky on fire / And no one here can break the spell
When the red nation pulls together / They gonna raise holy hell

— ROBBIE ROBERTSON

ALFRED J. KEYE ~

Alfred J. Keye entered the Longhouse in the arms of his mother. The infant son of staunch followers of the Longhouse traditions was given the name Ta wen ae, because, as Alfred puts it, "no one else was using it and it was handy." At sixteen, Alfred became a faithkeeper and, with other Longhouse faithkeepers, took on the responsibility for the upkeep of the Longhouse and its surroundings and the preparations for the ceremonies. He took on the task of ensuring that everyone attending the ceremonies understood what was unfolding. This involved translating for those who did not know the language. It involved teaching.

Alfred himself had good teachers. His father knew the Great Law, and his language and knowledge allowed him to do the ceremonies, including the Condolence Ceremony. His uncle, a Seneca and a Longhouse learned who spoke fluent Cayuga, sat beside Alfred in Council and explained the proceedings to the young boy.

Now, the man named Ta wen ae, which means "Words I Left Behind," leaves his words behind him every day. He leaves them in the minds of his students. They are words in the Cayuga language. He teaches his students about the Great Law and why it was given to the Iroquois. He teaches the new generation as he was taught and leaves behind these words: "The Great Law came down to us because we were fighting and killing each other. The Creator gave us the power to think, the power to think of different ways of getting round these difficulties, to negotiate, to become friends rather than enemies."

Alfred dances at pow-wow gatherings. This is an act that places him at variance with the view, held by some, that pow-wow dancing has no history with the Iroquois, being a celebration borrowed from the Plains Indians, and best left with them, in favor of the social dances. To that he responds: "In our culture, we are told that each of us is given something special, a gift. Mine is the gift of dance, and our culture tells us that we should share our gifts."

LEROY HILL ~ Leroy Hill is learning to speak. He is studying the ceremonial speeches of the Longhouse with his friend and mentor, Peter Sky. Together, they examine the philosophical ideas that are the wellspring for the speeches Leroy will one day present in Cayuga, the language of his childhood.

Leroy's boyhood friend was the son of a carver, Jake Thomas. The boys loved to watch as the stone was chiseled, filed, and polished. Waiting to see what emerged was a mesmerizing pastime. Jake gave them some "scraps" and encouraged them to try. With that, Leroy was launched on his life's work.

He learned by doing, and he learned well. He learned to carve intricate scenes that depict the legends associated with Iroquois ceremonies, the Creation Story, and the Great Law. Then, he learned how to sell.

When Leroy does take a break from sculpting in stone, he turns to welding. He likes the variety. One might guess that he enjoys how amenable metal can be to change when it is warmed. He welds and he waits for the next legend that will be revealed in stone.

Leroy, a Cayuga of the Bear Clan, is named Ho hah hays, which means "Long Path."

LANCE HODAHKWEN ~ Born on the Onondaga Reservation in

New York State, Lance received his name, Hodahkwen, during the Midwinter Ceremonies at the Onondaga Longhouse.

At twenty, he enlisted in the Air Force and went to Vietnam. As an air controller, he issued the "clear to land" signal for countless American pilots. His four years of service earned him an education under the GI bill. Following his discharge, he enrolled at Arizona State University for an undergraduate degree, majoring in education, and then went to the University of Oklahoma for a Master's degree in Public Health Administration.

Now, after a thirty-year career as a health systems administrator with Indian Health Services, Lance is anticipating a retirement that will let him attend a few more pow-wow gatherings to do a little dancing and a lot of visiting. He lives in the state of Maryland and travels home to the Onondaga Reservation for Longhouse ceremonies.

Lance Hodahkwen is an Onondaga of the Wolf Clan. Hodahkwen means "Runs Away."